Binational Collaboration in Health Insurance Services between the United States and Mexico: Issues and Innovations for the Texas Health Insurance Industry

by

Jeffrey John Stys

Special Project Report
Lyndon B. Johnson School of Public Affairs
The University of Texas at Austin

This report was originally presented by Jeffrey John Stys to the faculty of the Graduate School of the University of Texas at Austin in partial fulfillment of the requirements for the degree of Master of Public Affairs, The University of Texas at Austin (December 1995).

Library of Congress Catalog Card No.: 96-77888
ISBN: 0-89940-903-2

Cover design by Doug Marshall, LBJ School Publications Office

Contents

Tables

Acknowledgements

Many individuals aided in the preparation of this report. I would like to thank the Innovations in Insurance Fellowship Committee for funding my research. Additional financial support was provided by the Flora and William Hewlett Foundation and the Lyndon B. Johnson School of Public Affairs U.S.-Mexican Policy Studies Program. I would also like to acknowledge Richard Hoffman, of Blue Cross and Blue Shield of Texas, for his help in all of my endeavors, both academic and personal. Dr. David Warner provided me with the necessary guidance and criticism essential to the report. Birny Birnbaum and Gloria Leal both provided me with indispensable help in developing and conducting the survey of the Texas health insurance companies. Dr. Jose R. Antú, Director of the Buenavida Health Education Program for the City of Laredo health department, helped arrange my interviews in Laredo and Nuevo Laredo. Jane Barwell, who edited this report, provided me with criticism and encouragement, which greatly improved the final version of this report. Finally, I would like to thank my family and friends in New York and Texas. Your continued support and love means more to me than you could ever know.

Abstract

This report examines the relevant issues and implications for the Texas health insurance industry resulting from increased interaction with Mexican medical providers and insurance companies. Two distinct forms of cooperation and their potential for long-term effects on health care delivery in both countries are discussed. First, the report examines joint ventures between Texas and Mexican insurance companies. Second, the report explores the possibility of establishing cross-border health maintenance or preferred provider organizations. The report also includes an overview of the Mexican health care delivery system and an analysis of potential reforms, and it describes the role of private health insurance in the financing of health care in Mexico. The results of a survey of all health insurance companies licensed in Texas on their proposed and current activity in Mexico is also included.

Chapter 1. Introduction

In the era of the North American Free Trade Agreement (NAFTA), new and innovative alliances and agreements will emerge between individuals and companies in the United States and Mexico. Nationally, several health insurance companies are exploring previously unimagined collaborations with Mexican medical providers and insurance companies. This paper addresses cooperation between U.S. and Mexican providers and insurance companies and explores the possible long-term effects of cooperation on health care delivery in both countries.

With the recent passage of NAFTA, the potential for increased and sustained exchange between the two countries in the health insurance industry has not been adequately addressed. With an increased focus on free trade, the United States and Mexico will continue to trade medical services. One area of cooperation, the development of joint ventures between U.S. and established Mexican insurance companies, has been fostered by NAFTA's relaxation of restrictions on foreign ownership of Mexican insurance companies. Another form of cooperation is the development of U.S.-based health maintenance organizations (HMOs) and preferred provider organizations (PPOs) along the U.S.-Mexican border that include the participation of Mexican doctors and hospitals. Several U.S.-based insurance companies are including Mexican providers as a means of offering their clients greater freedom of choice at substantial savings. This interaction could influence the development of private insurance plans in Mexico and the health care of Texans who live along the Texas-Mexico border.

Understanding the history and contemporary issues facing the Mexican health care delivery system is essential for individuals interested in developing relations with Mexican providers or companies. Chapter 2 of this report outlines the Mexican national health system by highlighting national expenditures on health care and the quality of available services and by explaining the role of public and private institutions in health care delivery. Unlike in the United States, in Mexico, the health care system is mainly publicly financed with little emphasis on private insurance. The Mexican social security system, which provides a large percentage of health care, is increasingly under public scrutiny to provide higher quality and more efficient care. In recent times, both public and private research institutions have called for reform of the health care delivery system. The suggested reforms would create a greater role for private health insurance and health care providers.

Chapter 3 provides an overview of private health insurance in Mexico. The chapter begins with a description of the private health insurance market and describes typical policies and premiums. The role of international coverage is also discussed as well as the methods several Texas hospitals are using to attract patients from Mexico. Health insurance regulations in Mexico and restrictions on foreign ownership of Mexican companies are provided, and the emergence of U.S.-Mexico collaborations and the obstacles facing these companies are also discussed. The chapter concludes with a case study of Blue Cross and Blue Shield of Texas' planned joint venture with a major Mexican insurer.

Chapter 4 explores current attempts by companies to use the Mexican health care delivery system by developing cross-border insurance plans and looks at the resulting benefits to the Texas border region. The chapter begins with an overview of demographics along the Texas-Mexico border and documents the area's lack of hospitals and medical providers. The chapter also chronicles several current initiatives by companies to develop cross-border HMOs and PPOs. Several of the fundamental issues involved in developing cross-border insurance plans are discussed, including malpractice and the accreditation of hospitals and medical schools. The chapter concludes with a case study of the cities of Laredo, Texas, and Nuevo Laredo, Tamaulipas which illustrates many of the issues addressed.

Chapter 5 presents results of a survey of all companies licensed to sell health insurance in Texas. The survey, conducted under the auspices of the Texas Department of Insurance, quantifies the current and planned activities of Texas health insurance companies in the Mexican health insurance market. The survey not only inquired about current and planned expansion in the Mexican health insurance market but also asked companies to identify obstacles to developing relations with Mexican companies and providers.

Chapter 2. The Mexican Health Care Delivery System and Potential Reforms

To understand the role of private health insurance in Mexico, an understanding of the Mexican health care delivery system is vital. Unlike in the United States, in Mexico the public sector finances the majority of health care. The system is straining under continued pressure as a growing population demands more complex and expensive medical procedures. Growth pressures, along with calls for reform of government health care institutions, could have long-term implications for the role of private health insurance. To understand a foreign medical care delivery system, we must examine the history and most recent developments in both public and private institutions.

Overview of the Mexican Health Care Delivery System

The Mexican health care delivery system is a mix of both public and private providers, although public organizations provide the majority of health care. Under the Mexican Constitution, health care is a right of all Mexican citizens. Article 23 of the Constitution mandates that health services be part of the social security system (Soberon, 1994, p. 1). Because the Mexican Constitution has explicitly recognized a right to health protection, it assigns a key role to the state in conducting national health policy (Frenk et al., 1994, p. 1,592). The national health care system is comprised of three main providers: public health services, social security, and private hospital and medical care. Government organizations provide the majority of health care in Mexico to different populations through the different providers. Public health services provide medical care to the uninsured, mainly the urban and rural poor with no formal employment. All formally employed Mexicans contribute to and are entitled to use the social security system for their health needs.

Table 2.1 lists the total amount spent on health care in 1992 in both the public and private sector. The Fundación Mexicana para la Salud (Mexican Health Foundation, FUNSALUD) reports that a total of between 4.82 and 5.73 percent of the Mexican gross national product was spent on health care in 1992 (1994a, p. 35). According to the report, private sector spending on health care is also increasing. Private spending estimates are based on two different national studies. For the private sector, the low estimate was based on an analysis of the Encuesta Nacionales de Ingresos y Gastos de los Hogares (national survey of household income and expenditures). The high estimate was based on information from the Sistema de Cuentas Nacionales (system of national accounts). The total expenditures are listed in pesos and dollars to make international comparisons easier.

Table 2.1
Public and Private Medical Expenditures, 1992
(in millions of nuevos pesos and dollars)

Expenditure	Total Expenditure		Expenditure per Person		Percent of GNP
	N$	Dollars*	N$	Dollars*	
Public	28,559.5	9,211.3	329.1	106.2	2.76
Private: Low Estimate	21,283.4	6,864.5	245.3	79.1	2.06
Private: High Estimate	30,691.6	9,900.5	353.8	114.1	2.97
Total Low Estimate	49,842.9	16,075.0	574.4	185.3	4.82
Total High Estimate	59,256.1	19,111.8	682.9	220.2	5.73

Source: Adapted from Fundación Mexicana para la Salud, *Economía y Salud: Propuestas para el Avance del Sistema de Salud en México, Informe Final.*

*Based on the average exchange rate in 1992 of 3.1005 pesos per dollar

Public Health Services

Government institutions provide services to the noninsured population, those who do not have formal employment and therefore do not have access to social security institutions. These populations are mainly the urban and rural poor. Public health care services are provided by the Ministry of Health, the National Institutes of Health, and the Health Services of the Federal District. These publicly financed organizations and institutions serve approximately 30 percent of the population (Hernandez, 1994).

Social Security Institutions

This component of the national health system covers workers from the formal (i.e., not underground "informal") private and public sector of the economy. The social security system in Mexico has developed its own network of hospitals and salaried personnel, thereby combining financing and delivery of services in a single agency. Almost 55 percent of the nation subscribes to a social security institution (Frenk, et al., 1994, p. 1,593). The following highlights the major social security institutions in Mexico (see table 2.2).

The Instituto Mexicano del Seguro Social (Mexican Social Security Institute, IMSS) is the largest health care and hospital institution, which covers private sector employees, retirees, and their families. IMSS also provides additional benefits to workers, such as discount stores, loans, and recreational facilities. IMSS serves a large portion of the Mexican population and had a annual budget of N$10.5 billion in 1992 (United Communications Group, 1993). IMSS has a tripartite revenue source, with workers contributing 25 percent, employers contributing 70 percent, and the federal government contributing 5 percent (National Academy of Medicine, Mexico, 1993, p. 36). The Mexican Congress passed legislation in July of 1993 that increases social security taxes. In effect, employers and workers will have paid three basic social security taxes by 1996: 11.8765 percent for health services, 9.6 percent for the pension fund, and 5 percent for housing (United Communications Group, 1993).

The Instituto de Seguridad y Servicios Sociales de los Trabajadores del Estado (Social Security Institute at the Service of the State Workers, ISSSTE) insures government employees. Revenue comes from employee contributions amounting to 8 percent of wages. The federal government contributes the equivalent of 17.75 percent of workers' incomes (National Academy of Medicine, Mexico, 1993, p. 36). Other separate organizations provide care to some local government employees, the armed forces and the employees of Petroleos Mexicanos (PEMEX).

Table 2.2
Public Sector Medical Facilities, 1992

Institution	General Hospitals	Specialty Hospitals	Outpatient Units	Total
Secretariat of Health	178	49	6,790	7,017
IMSS-Solidarity	275	39	4,773	5,087
ISSSTE	77	10	1,093	1,180
Secretariat of National Defense	26	0	217	243
Secretariat of Navy	27	0	95	122
PEMEX	15	8	168	191
Federal District Dept.	14	17	106	137
State	64	34	97	195
Total	**676**	**157**	**6,790**	**14,172**

Source: Adapted from International Medical Associates, Inc., "Opportunities for U.S. Participation in the Expansion of the Mexican Health Care System."

Private Medical Care in Mexico

Private health services in Mexico are heterogeneous. Facilities range from high quality to those that provide only the most basic services. In a 1993 survey of private hospitals in Mexico, hospitals were categorized "high," "medium," or "low complexity" depending on the total number of beds. Of Mexico's 2,165 private hospitals, only 10 percent were classified as high complexity, reporting 60 beds or more (Hurtado-Belendez, 1994a). Seventy percent of the hospitals had up to 10 beds which was considered low complexity. The remaining 20 percent had 11 to 59 beds, considered medium complexity institutions. In a census of available facilities, there were 472 private hospitals with 15 beds or more; these institutions provided a combined total of 17,707 available beds (FUNSALUD, 1994a, p. 36). About 30 percent of Mexicans, mainly upper- and middle-class individuals who may have qualified for medical services through social security, chose to use private services (Soberon, 1994, p. 3).

Problems in the Social Security System

The Instituto Mexicano del Seguro Social is faced with serious problems, according to a recently published analysis of the system. The analysis was requested by President Ernesto Zedillo in 1995, as the basis for discussion to generate opinions and proposals for IMSS reforms. In an interview in the Mexican magazine *Epoca*, Genero Borrego, IMSS general director, stated that the analysis recognizes IMSS strengths but also acknowledges its weaknesses, failures, and errors. IMSS is plagued by structural financial and administrative problems ("El Diagnóstico Reconoce Debilidades," 1995, p. 16). External pressures from the increasing number of elderly in Mexico, whose medical care is more expensive than that of the young, have placed additional burdens on the system. For every ten workers affiliated with IMSS, there are 1.4 elderly persons (Sánchez, 1995, p. 8).

The IMSS medical system has been described as a "labyrinth of inefficiency," characterized by long waiting periods, diagnostic test deferrals, and lack of medicines as well as shortages and obsolescence of equipment (Moreno and Cruz, 1995, p. 10). The health care delivery system of IMSS is separated into three distinct levels and each level faces serious problems. The first level, commonly called family practice, provides primary care and serves as an entry point to the rest of the system. Clients are reported to be dissatisfied with the impersonal treatment and lack of reliable patient-doctor relationships at this level. Physicians employed in the public sector are expected to see 40 patients in an eight-hour day (Hurtado-Belendez, 1994b). According to Dr. Rogelio Martinez-Banuet, who works in both the public and private systems, a patient must go through a complex series of referrals before the patient can be seen by a specialist in the public system (1994). There is no system to appraise the quality of the performance of doctors, who often spend a significant part of their time performing clerical duties.

At the second level, patients are referred to a general hospital where procedures such as those requiring medical specialty, inpatient surgery, and specialized treatment are performed. This level is faced with problems of inadequate planning and administration. Administrators are not allowed to allocate resources to meet pressing needs, because they are limited to minor modifications of programs established at centralized agencies. Serious work overloads also occur in some areas because labor contracts, accompanied by high rates of absenteeism, do not allow labor shortages in one unit to be filled with personnel from another.

The third level is made up of 42 high-specialty hospitals, which treat more serious illnesses requiring specialized medical and complex technical resources. This level not only faces problems of inadequate planning and administration but also has serious shortages of medicines and diagnostic equipment. Because of the administrative problems at the first two levels, illnesses that should be treated at the primary or intermediate levels of care are treated at the third level, which raises costs and misallocates resources.

Although reforms of the social security system have been discussed in the public and private sectors, no concrete proposals have yet been offered by government officials. One of the conditions established by the president when calling for the analysis of IMSS was that it not be privatized ("El Diagnóstico Reconoce Debilidades," 1995, p. 16). One alternative to outright privatization is the creation of alternative social security plans. Under such plans, the IMSS would remain under the state's control, but private administrators would control pension funds and health insurance plans. Workers could then choose between substitute health care insurance plans or remain under IMSS. These substitute organizations would be financed in a similar fashion as an official institution, being supported by employer and employee contributions and general taxes. This will not be an easy task due to the constitutionality of the benefits granted to the workers of IMSS (Sánchez, 1995, p. 8).

Calls for Reform of the National Health Care Delivery System

Social, economic, demographic, and epidemiological forces are changing the Mexican health care system. Mexico experienced an increasing gross domestic product per capital from $1,831 in 1987 to $4,204 in 1993 (Ramírez de Alba, 1994). Prior to the recent economic crisis, the demand for private health care had been growing as the Mexican economy had expanded. Wealthy and middle-class Mexicans prefer private health services to avoid the delays and impersonal attention at government-run institutions. Although the recent devaluation of the peso may temporarily lessen the demand for these services, there will be a continued demand for private health care as the Mexican economy improves.

In the past 20 years Mexico has seen a declining birth rate, which will eventually result in an older population faced with chronic diseases that are more expensive to treat. Mexico has also experienced epidemiological changes, which can be characterized by four factors:

1. the transition from a predominance of common infections and malnutrition as the leading causes of death to a preponderance of noncommunicable diseases, injuries and new infections;

2. a shift in importance from child to adult mortality, especially among the elderly;

3. a relative predominance of morbidity over mortality in defining the overall health picture of the population, and

4. a change in the social meaning of disease, which ceases to be an acute event that is resolved when the patient either is cured or dies (Frenk, 1994b, p. 3).

The North American Free Trade Agreement (NAFTA) is expected to accelerate the process of privatization of medical services (Soberon, 1994, p. 3). The Fundación Mexicana para la Salud conducted a year-long study directed by Dr. Julio Frenk, former director of the Instituto Nacional de Salud Pública (National Institute of Public Health of Mexico), to provide a conceptual framework for the reformed system. FUNSALUD's recommendations include complete decentralization of the public health care system, separate financing and delivery of services, and organization of the health service by function rather than by segmented population. Within this newly envisioned system, the Secretaría de Salud (secretary of health) would continue to regulate the health care system. Financing in the new system would take advantage of social security's experience but would also be open to new options that include private insurance or special funds. The delivery of services would be open to participation of both the private and public sectors on a competitive basis, which grants consumers freedom of choice (Soberon, 1994, p. 4).

The recommendations in FUNSALUD's proposal included a role for private health insurance and challenged the often-taken-for-granted role of the social security system as a major health service deliverer. The proposal recommends that social security should remain a major funder of services, but there should also be a role for private insurance. Within the reformed system, private insurance would play a greater synergistic role as a means of financing medical services. The proposal calls for other institutions to provide services if they can do so more efficiently and with higher quality. Also, within the new health care system, private insurance would provide greater freedom for individuals and businesses to acquire different types of insurance and establish incentives for the design of innovative models of private insurance. Currently, people who have rights to the social security system but are using private services are, in effect, paying twice for medical services (FUNSALUD, 1994a, pp. 230-32).

According to FUNSALUD's proposal, new forms of private participation will be needed in the reformed system. The State will focus on the creation of a clear vision of the values, the principles, and the purpose of the national health system. The private sector, using its considerable experience, could apply its talents to the creation of options for the population. NAFTA is expected to bring not only investment in private health insurance but also multiple opportunities for Mexico to adopt such innovations as prepaid insurance plans, managerial information systems, and quality assurance programs. Although FUNSALUD's proposal admits the possibility that inefficient forms of health care financing might be introduced, it concludes that the opportunities that would result from the harmonization of Mexico's regulatory insurance standards with those of the United States and Canada would outweigh the risks (FUNSALUD, 1994a, pp. 245-46).

Private Hospital Development in Mexico

Increased demand for private medical services has led to expanded development of private health care facilities throughout Mexico. As the level of service decreases and the waiting periods increase at government-run institutions, wealthy and middle-class Mexican are increasingly using private doctors and hospitals. With the passage of NAFTA, there has been interest within the U.S. medical industry in participating in the expansion of the Mexican health care industry through the exchanging of personnel, training, and the building and managing of health care centers. There are more than 60 cities in Mexico with populations greater than 100,000, and many of these cities do not have high-quality medical facilities (Bennett, 1994). One recent study estimates that there will need to be at least 30 tertiary, or specialty, hospitals of more than 100 beds each developed over the next ten years in Mexico (International Medical Associates, 1994, p. 5).

Although there were no legal restrictions on investment in medical facilities in Mexico the passage of NAFTA has helped increase interest in health services in Mexico. Frenk and his colleagues acknowledge the potential benefits and drawbacks from foreign participation in the health field in Mexico. "Foreign units can satisfy unmet needs, create jobs, decrease capital flight by reducing the number of Mexican consumers seeking health care abroad, promote competition beneficial to consumers, and introduce efficient models of service delivery and managerial technology (cost accounting, prepayment systems, etc.)." The article does admit there are potential drawbacks that could result in patient discrimination and unnecessary procedures. To have a positive impact on the health system, Mexico will require that effective means of ensuring equity, quality, and cost containment be in place before the market opens (1994, p. 1,595).

Domestic and foreign hospitals are planning to expand existing facilities or construct new facilities to meet the growing demand for private health care services. Demand for higher quality medical care is expected to continue to grow with the improvement of the general economy and continued public dissatisfaction with government-run hospitals (International Medical Associates, 1994, p. 16). Table 2.3 lists the current expansion of medical facilities in Mexico.

Table 2.3
Mexican Hospital Projects

Hospital Name	# Beds	U.S. Participant	City	Project Status
Hermosillo	75	International Hospital Corp.	Hermosillo, Son.	Construction Complete
Chihuahua	55	International Hospital Corp.	Chihuahua, Chi.	Under Construction
Centro Medico Excel		Alvarado Hospital	Tijuana, B. C.	Under Construction
H. San Juan Bautista	70	?	Villahermosa, Ta.	Under Construction
Centro Culiacan	75	?	Culiacan, Sin.	Planning
Hospital A.B.C.	>150	?	Mexico City	Planning
Scripps Aguascalientes	80	ScrippsHealth	Aguascalientes, Ag.	Postponed
Sharp Hospital Mazatlan	110	Sharp Health	Mazatlan, Sin.	Under Construction
Hospital Providencia	60	HELTHSRV*	Guadalajara, Jal.	Building Permit
Hospital Angel Leano	150	?	Guadalajara, Jal.	Planning
Angeles Del Pedregal	200	?	Mexico City	Planning
Mercy Hospital	80	?	Guadalajara, Jal.	Replanning
Centro Medico de Colima	80	HELTHSRV*	Colima, Co.	Under Construction

Sources: Adapted from International Medical Associates, Inc., "Opportunities for U.S. Participation in the Expansion of the Mexican Health Care System"; Lawrence Meagher, President and CEO of the International Hospital Corporation, telephone interview, May 22, 1995; and Steven Goe, Vice President International Markets, ScrippsHealth, La Jolla, Calif., telephone interview, July 10, 1995.

*HELTHSRV is based in Calgary, Alberta, Canada.

Private health insurance may play a major role in not only the financing of medical care at these new facilities but also the development of cost containment, innovative prepayment plans, and hospital and physician credentialing. Lawrence Meagher, president and CEO of the International Hospital Corporation, believes that a mutually beneficial relationship will develop between Mexican health insurance companies and new hospital facilities in Mexico (1995a). Newly opened Mexican hospitals can help Mexican insurance companies expand their products and explore managed care concepts. With almost no standardization of hospital records and reliable sources of data, insurance companies do not have the information necessary to make decisions on fees and premiums. Presently throughout Mexico there is no standardization of hospital records, and often, the only available information is doctors' orders and nurses' notes. Some Mexican insurance companies have made some attempts to ensure that services were actually performed. Yet, these same companies have not implemented systems to analyze the effectiveness of these services. The hospitals can help with the development of protocols through the establishment of coding systems and admitting and discharge diagnoses (Meagher, 1995a).

Private health insurers, especially those from the United States, will need criteria for choosing hospitals with which to affiliate. Until recently, no hospital certification system existed in Mexico. There was no private organization similar to the Joint Commission on Accreditation of Health Care Services (JCAHO) in the United States (Warner and Reed, 1993, p. 94). The Mexican Commission on Certification of Health Care Services has recommended only first stage, rudimentary standards for all hospital units and expects to be granted the role of accrediting organization by government officials (Hurtado-Belendez, 1994a). Insurance companies will also need to develop criteria for choosing physicians with whom to work. The training of physicians and the varying quality of private health institutions are discussed in chapter 4.

Current Hospital Development in Mexico

Fourteen hospitals, with a total of 1,200 beds are currently under construction in Mexico (International Medical Associates, 1994, p. 24). This hospital development represents not only an improvement in the facilities in Mexico but a substantial amount of revenue for U.S. exporters as well. The estimated cost of equipment to be imported from the United States for an 80-bed community hospital in Mexico is $11,645,901, or $145,686 per bed (International Medical Associates, 1994, p. 22). The International Hospital Corporation is the industry leader in Mexican hospital development. Another U.S.-based international development corporation, GroupMed, has entered into a contractual relationship with Grupo Situr to develop 20 health campuses throughout Mexico (International Medical Associates, 1994, p. 49).

Formed in 1991, International Hospital Corporation is building private, for-profit hospitals in Hermosillo, Chihuahua, and Puebla. The 75-bed facility in Hermosillo, costing about $25 million, is scheduled to open August 1, 1995, and the 54-bed facility in Chihuahua is expected to open in early 1996 (Meagher, 1995b). International Hospital Corporation contributes about one-third of the equity of each of the hospitals, and

Mexican partners, primarily local business people and the physicians who will work at the facilities, invest the other two-thirds. Physicians who will work at the facilities also have a stake in making the hospital efficient and profitable. According to cofounder Gary Woods, International Hospital Corporation plans to open other facilities at the rate of about one every six months, beginning after the opening of the hospitals in Hermosillo and Chihuahua (Deener, 1994, p. 1D).

GroupMed, along with Grupo Situr, plans to develop more than 20 health-related campuses within Situr's megadevelopment areas throughout Mexico over the next several years. These campuses will be situated on Situr's and other major tourist-related developments, which will also include marinas, hotels, airstrips, and condominiums. GroupMed plans to incorporate its own health spas, medical facilities, and related health housing into these developments.

Specifically, GroupMed, working in conjunction with major regional and U.S. hospital development teams, will provide medical care and facilities for the entire project, with the U.S. hospitals working in consultation with Mexican medical teams. Quality medical facilities will enhance the attractiveness of GroupMed sites as retirement or vacation destinations, especially for foreign retirees who currently are wary of traveling or residing in such areas because of the uncertainty of emergency medical care facilities. GroupMed has initiated its first location for development at Situr's BajaMar Golf and Resort Club, 55 miles south of San Diego. GroupMed has purchased an area of more than 18 acres for its medical clinic and related housing. Twenty miles away in Ensenada, the Hospital Las Americas will provide necessary tertiary care, and U.S. patients will also have the option of transferring to San Diego for further care (International Medical Associates, 1994, pp. 49-51).

Conclusion

A fundamental understanding of the health care delivery system is essential for companies interested in expanding services in Mexico. Mexican government institutions play a major role in health care delivery. Any reform of the public system will have long-term effects on the health care delivery system of Mexico. The internal pressure for change along with the entrance of foreign medical institutions will influence health care and private health insurance in Mexico. Greater individual choice in the selection of health plans will create opportunities for insurance companies familiar with Mexican medical services to develop new products and services.

Chapter 3. Private Health Insurance In Mexico

Compared to the United States, the Mexican health insurance industry is in its relative infancy. Mexican health insurers began to sell policies in the 1980s, and the number of policies sold grew from 242,000 in 1987 to 533,000 in 1989 (Laurell and Ortega, 1992, p. 334). Traditionally, health insurance has been a relatively small product line in the overall Mexican insurance industry, and insurers have faced continued losses on health policies. As the number of policies has increased, insurance companies have attempted to combat losses by instituting increased deductibles, implementing catalog and fee schedules, and establishing preferred provider organizations (Torres Cross, 1992, p. 31). Foreign insurance companies view Mexico as a growth market for private insurance as demand for private services grows, and as a prime target for instituting managed care principles as a way of controlling health care costs. Although the health insurance market is not as developed in Mexico as it is the United States, the entrance of foreign insurance firms may have long-lasting effects on the development of private insurance plans in Mexico.

The Mexican Health Insurance Industry

Despite Mexico's dramatic growth in the last ten years, the country is one of the most underinsured nations in the world insurance market. According to Mexico's National Insurance Commission, spending on all insurance premiums amounts to the equivalent of $30 per capita, or 1.3 percent of the gross domestic product. This compares to the total insurance spending in the United States of $1,822 per capita, or 8.9 percent of the gross domestic product (SourceMex, 1993a). The International Insurance Council in Washington, D.C., found the Mexican market growing much faster than the U.S. domestic market and expects the situation to continue over the next few years ("Scramble for Places," 1993, p. 4). Prior to the December 1994 devaluation of the peso, foreign insurers hoped that, as the Mexican economy improved, Mexicans, especially the growing middle-class, could be persuaded to develop a taste for insurance ("Why Insurers Are Splashing," 1993, p. 68).

Of the 20 Mexican insurance companies currently writing health insurance policies, 5 companies control over 75 percent of the health insurance market. Table 3.1 illustrates the distribution of the total insurance market share and health insurance market share of the top companies.

The concept of private health insurance is not widespread in Mexico. The current Mexican private health insurance market is extremely small relative to the market size in the United States. Even though most Mexican employees are entitled to health care under the government system, many higher paid employees choose to seek private health care for a variety of reasons. Because of the preference for private physicians and hospitals, supplemental employer-sponsored medical plans are popular for high-level employees.

One hundred percent of the employer's insurance cost is tax deductible if coverage is provided for all employees (William M. Mercer, 1992, p. 41). Often, employers will form subsidiary companies comprised only of executives for the sole purpose of being able to deduct the entire cost of executive health insurance premiums (Aguilar, 1994).

Table 3.1
Domestic Market Share of Mexican Health Insurance Industry, Year End 1993

Company	**Total Insurance Market Share**	**Health Insurance Market Share**
Grupo Nacional Provincial	19.96%	29.93%
Commercial America	19.59%	21.65%
Monterrey	12.88%	11.33%
Asemex	12.77%	7.24%
Segumex	9.27%	5.64%
Total	**74.47%**	**75.54%**

Source: Adapted from Asociación Mexicana de Instituciones de Seguros, *Estadística de Primas y Siniestros Directos Acumulados.*

While health insurance has, until now, been a relatively small product line in Mexico, it is presently one of the fastest growing lines. According to the leading health insurer in Mexico, the industry has grown 800 percent since 1988. Although this is an impressive statistic, only 5.5 percent of all Mexicans are covered by private health insurance (Rodriguez-Monroy, 1994). A typical policy in Mexico consists of a comprehensive major medical plan with 10 to 20 percent copays, $50 to $200 deductibles per illness, and a $2,500 to $1,000,000 maximum per illness (Miller, 1993, p. 10).

Table 3.2 illustrates rate schedules for the different policies from Grupo Nacional Provincial, which controls 29.93 percent of the Mexican health insurance market. The listed rates are for low- (Tradicional) and high-end (Premier) individual policies. Group policies are available based on the number of policies desired, with rates slightly cheaper than for individual policies. Table 3.2 also shows several of the options that are available on listed policies.

Table 3.2
Grupo Nacional Provincial Health Insurance Rates, 1994
(in new pesos)

	Plan Name			
	Tradicional		Premier	
Amount Insured	100 SMGM*	400 SMGM	600 SMGM	1000 SMGM
Coinsurance	10%	10%	10%	10%
Deductible	5 SMGM	5 SMGM	5 SMGM	5 SMGM
Annual Premium for				
30-year-old male	N$572	N$662	N$1,081	N$1,146
30-year-old female	N$796	N$925	N$1,525	N$1619
50-year-old male	N$1,204	N$1,404	N$2,334	N$2,480
50-year-old female	N$1,380	N$1,612	N$2,684	N$2,853

Source: Grupo Nacional Provincial, *Tarifas Gastos Medicos.*

*SMGM, or *salario minimo general mensual,* is the general monthly minimum salary set by the Mexican government. For the above information, the SMGM was set at N$458.10.

When choosing a policy from Grupo Nacional Provincial, the insured chooses from four different policies. For each plan, the individual chooses the maximum amount covered, the deductible, and coinsurance. Grupo Nacional Provincial has four different policies: Premier, Español, Clasica, and Tradicional. The policy chosen dictates at which hospitals the insured is eligible to receive services. The most expensive policy gives the insureds the opportunity to seek care at the nation's most prestigious hospital. If the insured seeks care at a hospital above the contracted level, there is an additional 20 percent coinsurance. The hospital network, Linea Azul Hospitalaria, operates at 95 percent of the principal private hospitals in the country (Rodriguez-Monroy, 1994). Grupo

Nacional Provincial offers the added incentive of eliminating the deductible when using hospitals within the network for planned surgeries.

International Coverage

Using patient origin data supplied by the Texas Hospital Association, Warner and Reed estimate that 5,600 persons with Mexican addresses were treated in Texas hospitals in both 1987-88 and 1988-89 (1993, p. 143). The study estimates that 1,300 to 1,400 were U.S. citizens, with the rest being Mexican nationals. Mexican nationals often seek more complex medical procedures in the United States. Several Texas hospitals have established programs to attract these patients and developed cooperative relationships with Mexican hospitals, hoping that Mexican physicians will refer patients to U.S. hospitals. Methodist Hospital in Houston has relationships with five Mexican hospitals for whom they have provided administrative assistance and educational programs (International Medical Associates, 1994, p. 31). Baylor University Medical Center in Houston has a long-standing agreement with a medical school in Monterrey and a pending relationship with the Instituto de Seguridad y Servicios Sociales de los Trabajadores del Estado (ISSSTE) for postgraduate training (International Medical Associates, 1994, p. 32).

Several Texas hospitals treat patients who have international health insurance coverage. Methodist Hospital has several alliances with Mexican insurance carriers (Nunez, 1995). Baylor Hospital in Dallas has agreements with Commercial America and Grupo Nacional Provincial (Hinojosa, 1995). Both hospitals require that patients go through a preapproval process, and Methodist requires that each patient present a letter of guarantee and a preadmission deposit to cover any copayment (Nunez, 1995).

Most Mexican insurance companies offer, or are planning to offer, international options on policies. These options offer treatment outside of Mexico with Texas and Florida as prime destinations. For example, Seguros Monterrey offers three different levels of international coverage. For this coverage, all insured amounts, deductibles, coinsurance, and premiums are stated in U.S. dollars. All plans have maximum insured benefits of $2,000,000 and a 20 percent coinsurance with a maximum coinsurance contribution of $1,000. Within the United States, the deductible depends upon whether the insured uses established hospital networks. When using approved hospitals there is a $500, $1,250, or $2,500 deductible depending upon the plan chosen. Deductibles at nonnetwork hospitals range from $1,000 to $5,000. Table 3.3 illustrates the premiums, listed in dollars. The price of the policy depends upon the location where the policy is purchased.

International policy premiums are based on the probability of the individuals' utilizing the health care delivery system in the United States. The most expensive policies are sold in Zone I, which corresponds to cities bordering the United States. Zone II policies are sold in the areas outside of the border cities in all of the Mexican states that border the United States along with Baja California Sur. Zone III includes all other sections of

Mexico. The cities of Tampico, Torreón, and Ciudad Madero which are located in border states, are excluded from this zone because of the distance and difficulty of crossing into the United States.

Table 3.3
Rates for International Coverage from Seguros Monterrey
(in dollars)

	Zone I			Zone II			Zone III		
	A	B	C	A	B	C	A	B	C
Annual Premium for									
30-year-old male	1043	858	766	869	715	667	652	536	479
30-year-old female	1307	1142	937	1089	952	817	817	714	586
50-year-old male	1815	1564	1287	1513	1304	1121	1134	978	804
50-year-old female	2105	1742	1393	1755	1452	1213	1116	1089	870

Source: Seguros Monterrey Aetna, *Manual de Tarifas*.

InterCare: The First Mexican HMO

Among recent changes in the health care system in Mexico is the development of a health maintenance organization (HMO), InterCare. The project began in 1992 but was closed down five hours after it began because it was considered by government regulators to be a renegade organization. The project was revived in January 1993 and now has a network of 1,533 physicians and 41 hospitals. The HMO claimed to have almost 30,000 members in August of 1993. InterCare offers a prepaid medical plan which includes medical checkups, diagnostic tests and surgical services (Coronado, 1994).

Dr. Luis Coronado Gonzales, director general of InterCare, described several of the pitfalls in trying to establish an HMO in the Mexican market. First, he suggested that the Comisión Nacional de Seguros y Fianzas (National Insurance and Surety Commission, CNSF) lacks awareness of the goals and operation of HMOs, although the regulatory agency is constantly monitoring the organization. The second pitfall he identified is that Mexican doctors are reluctant to negotiate discounts for an assured flow of patients because they are accustomed to charging patients varying rates for the same service based on their ability to pay. Dr. Coronado also identified as a barrier the Mexican public's lack of appreciation for the importance of basic, preventive care. Finally, he suggested that most companies will resist paying any additional cost for private health insurance for their employees as long as they are required to pay social security for their workers (1994).

Regulation of Health Insurance in Mexico

Created in 1990, the Comisión Nacional de Seguros y Fianzas supervises operations and ensures that insurance companies comply with the laws set by the finance ministry. The CNSF supports the development of the insurance market along with regulation, and interacts with policyholders. The agency has strengthened its ability to monitor company solvency through state-of-the-art technology and is currently studying the creation of a state guarantee fund to protect Mexican policy holders ("NAFTA Effects," 1993, p. 1).

Several laws regulate all types of insurance in Mexico. The following lists the legislation and how it relates to insurance companies.

1. The Ley Sobre el Contrato de Seguro (insurance contract law) establishes the rights and obligations of the parties involved in an insurance contract.

2. The Ley General de Instituciones y Sociedades Mutualistas de Seguros (LGISM, general law of insurance companies and mutual societies) provides the legal framework for insurance companies concerning their organization, performance, accounting, inspection, and surveillance.

3. The Ley Federal de Instituciones de Fianzas (LFIF, federal law of surety firms) provides the legal framework for surety firms.

4. The Reglamento de Agentes de Seguros y Fianzas (insurance and surety agent regulation) regulates the scope and activities of insurance and surety agents (CNSF, 1995).

The legislative framework's authorization of the disclosure of financial statements and creation of investment regulations are among its most important functions. The LGISM sets the general principles, while the Secretaría de Hacienda y Crédito Público (SHCP, Ministry of the Treasury) and the Comisión Nacional de Seguros y Fianzas create and enforce the specific rules and requirements.

According to article 3 of the LGISM, it is currently illegal for non-Mexican insurance firms to sell health insurance to Mexican citizens for coverage in Mexico (CNSF, 1994, p. 1). Traditionally, the only way for a foreign company to enter the Mexican market has been through a joint venture or partnership with a Mexican company authorized by the SHCP. Provisions of NAFTA will gradually increase the maximum amount of foreign joint-venture ownership, until complete foreign ownership is permitted by the year 2000. Despite the legal restrictions, there are definite advantages to developing joint ventures with established insurance institutions. Any joint venture should capitalize on complementary resources from each partner and also reduce risk and enhance mutual commitment.

Table 3.4 illustrates many of the qualities that each company can bring to a relationship. Although the table illustrates joint-venture partnerships in traditional health care projects, the concepts can be adapted for the insurance industry. An experienced Mexican partner contributes necessary operational experience with physicians and hospitals, and familiarity with the regulation of health insurance. A U.S. partner will bring additional financing, experience in managing medical costs, and superior access to computer networks and software.

Table 3.4
Contributions of Joint Venture Partners

Mexican Partner	U.S. Partner
Capital/Financing	Capital/Financing
Physician Groups	Access to International Coverage
Market Knowledge and Access	Operating Systems
Legal Expertise	Accreditation Knowledge
Community Leaders	Managed Care Concepts
Local Business Knowledge	Software

Source: Adapted from Russell A. Bennett, "Desirable Types of Projects and Joint Venture Projects," paper presented at a conference on "Health Care in Mexico: Infrastructure, Technologies and Financing: Challenges and Opportunities," La Jolla, Calif. (July 18, 1994).

Joint Ventures between U.S. and Mexican Insurance Companies

Several American and foreign insurance firms see Mexico as a promising new market for health insurance products. American firms have been investing in existing Mexican firms to ease entrance in the market. Table 3.5 shows current foreign investment in Mexican insurance companies. U.S. companies have expertise in marketing and technology and the experience to help the Mexican insurance industry develop into a more mature industry.

Dr. Julio Frenk, Director of Fundación Mexicana para la Salud, believes the industry needs to mature, not simply to grow. He questions whether the market will develop from an industry that offers a single indemnity product covering a small percentage of the population to a more innovated and developed one, offering a wider variety of products to a larger portion of the population (1995).

Table 3.5
American Investment in Mexican Insurance Companies, 1993

Mexican Insurance Company	American Investor	% American Ownership
Seguros Monterrey	Aetna	44.5
Seguros Interamericana	AIG	49.0
Seguros Genesis	Met Life	30.0
Seguros Cigna	Cigna	30.0
Seguros Protección Mutua	Reliance	30.0
Seguros Equitativa	Chubb	30.0
Geo New York Life	New York Life	30.0

Source: Adapted from Asociación Mexicana de Instituciones de Seguros, *El Seguro Mexicano,* and SourceMex, "U.S. Companies Form Partnerships with Mexican Firms to Gain Access to Latin American Insurance Market."

Limitations on Investment

Current regulations prohibit a foreign insurance company from acquiring more than 30 percent of a Mexican insurance company, although this percentage can be increased to 49 percent if approval is given by the Comisión Nacional de Seguros y Fianzas. Under NAFTA, American and Canadian insurers new to Mexico will be able to form joint ventures with Mexican partners, with controlling interests of 30 percent in 1994, rising to 35 percent in 1995, 40 percent in 1996, 45 percent in 1997, 51 percent in 1998, 75 percent in 1999, and 100 percent by the year 2000 (Dykewicz, 1993, p. 7A).

By limiting maximum investment by foreign firms, Mexican insurance regulations also prevent foreign-based insurance companies from controlling more than a predetermined percentage of the total domestic insurance market. According to the *Diario Oficial* of May 27, 1994, the maximum amount that a foreign insurance company can invest in a health insurance company is N$58,937,705. Table 3.6 lists the maximum allowed percentages of foreign investment in all Mexican insurance companies, including health insurers, according to NAFTA.

Table 3.6
Allowed Percentage of Investment by Foreign Firms in Mexican Insurance Companies

Date	Percent of Total Capital
January 1, 1994	6
January 1, 1995	8
January 1, 1996	9
January 1, 1997	10
January 1, 1998	11
January 1, 1999	12

Source: Lista de Mexico, *Trato de Libre Comercio, Anexo VII.*

Issues for U.S. Investment in the Mexican Health Insurance Market

American companies face imposing obstacles when trying to market private health insurance products. Because the majority of Mexicans have rights to use the public health system, private health insurance is a relatively new concept in Mexico. The novelty of private health insurance and structural conditions of the private health care system will make developing insurance products more difficult. Medical fees rose 27.5 percent in 1992 and hospitalization costs rose 29.56 percent in the same period (Rodriguez-Monroy, 1994). The overall medical inflation rate for pharmaceuticals and hospitals in 1994 was 9.8 percent and is expected to be more than 50 percent in 1995 (William M. Mercer, 1995). There is also resistance from some doctors and hospitals to accept insurance patients because they are accustomed to charging according to the patient's ability to pay.

One of the greatest challenges facing health insurers is the lack of reliable statistics. Grupo Nacional Provincial, the leading health insurance company, began a concerted effort to collect sufficient data to aid in controlling high loss ratios. Although the company began the effort to collect reliable data in 1991, the company did not begin using diagnosis-related groups until 1994.

One positive development in this area are standardized reporting forms to be given to the CSNF which are being developed through the Asociación Mexicana de Instituciones de Seguros (Association of Mexican Insurance Institutions, AMIS). This industry group, with 38 affiliated companies, believes its mission is to provide reliable statistics for all lines of Mexican insurance (AMIS, 1993a, p. 4).

AMIS believes that the entrance of foreign insurance companies will be an important step in the creation of reliable systems to collect statistical data (Armenta, 1994). In cooperation with the CNSF, AMIS has worked through technical committees to develop a new reporting system known as Sistema Estadístico del Sector Aseguradora, or SESA (statistical system of the insurance sector). By 1995 all insurance companies must use this more concise and encompassing reporting system. Under the previous reporting system, only total premiums, number of effective policies, and loss-ratio statistics were reported in composite form. Under the new system, policies are reported by age and sex of the policyholder and state where the policy was issued. The new system will present a more detailed picture of the overall insurance market in Mexico.

Blue Cross and Blue Shield of Texas and Aseguradora Mexicana

In July 1993, the Blue Cross and Blue Shield Association (BCBSA) issued a request for information to interested Blue Cross and Blue Shield Plans for the licensing of the Blue Cross and Blue Shield name and trademark in Mexico. Even though Congress had not yet passed NAFTA, BCBSA believed that Mexican government efforts to attract foreign investment provided an excellent opportunity for a Blue Cross and Blue Shield plan. Blue Cross and Blue Shield of Texas (BCBSTX) along with Blue Cross and Blue Shield of Arizona (BCBSAZ) responded to the request for information and were subsequently awarded the rights to use the Blue Cross and Blue Shield name and trademark in Mexico. During the time that followed the request for information, BCBSTX and BCBSAZ negotiated with Aseguradora Mexicana (Asemex), a well-known Mexican insurance company, to form a new company known as Blue Cross and Blue Shield of Mexico (BCBSMX).

With the lack of diversified insurance products in the Mexican market, and the increased demand for private medical services, both the Texas and Arizona Blue Cross and Blue Shield plans believed that there was great growth potential in the Mexican health insurance market. The companies planned to develop and market several different products designed to attract both individuals and groups in Mexico. The plans believed they could provide well-designed products to affluent Mexicans and the growing middle-class. The plans also believed that the U.S. expatriate community and the employees of *maquiladoras* located near the U.S. border were untapped markets.

Acknowledging the legal restrictions and their lack of knowledge of Mexican health insurance, the two Blue Cross and Blue Shield plans wanted to find an experienced and philosophically compatible Mexican partner to ease their entrance into the market. The plans actively negotiated with Aseguradora Mexicana following the request for information and planned to enter into a joint-venture agreement in January of 1995.

The Mexican economic crisis of December 1994 did not deter the Blue Cross and Blue Shield plans from their proposed investment, although the plans saw the middle-class, one of their potential markets, practically disappear overnight. Interest rates on mortgages, credit cards and car loans reached 90 percent or higher, greatly diminishing discretionary income of middle-class Mexicans (DePalma, 1995, p. 4). This severe economic news did not initially prevent investment plans but led to a focus on different opportunities in the market.

The decision to enter into an agreement, however, was indefinitely postponed. The financial group, Asemex-Banpais, which owned Asemex, was placed under the managerial control of The Comisión Nacional Bancaria (National Banking Commission) and the Comisión Nacional de Seguros y Fianzas on March 3, 1995, due to Asemex-Banpais' lack of adequate capital and financial reserves. According to Mexican insurance insiders, Asemex is a financially sound company and the current problems facing the financial group are due to Banpais' lack of adequate capital and reserves ("World Corporate Insurance Reports," 1995). The Blue Cross plans believe that a joint-venture agreement with Asemex could be completed within the next year.

Conclusion

Although private health insurance in Mexico has grown rapidly in the past few years, it has not fully developed into a major financing mechanism for health care. The combined influence of internal pressure and foreign insurance carriers entering the market will have long-lasting effects on private health insurance and the medical system in Mexico. New developments of HMOs and other innovative prepayment plans will influence the financing of Mexican health care. Foreign companies wishing to enter the market need to understand the limitations imposed by government regulators and market conditions. Although the potential exists for foreign companies to enter the market, such companies will face barriers and should be flexible when developing products and premiums and when interacting with providers and clients.

Chapter 4. Developing HMOs and PPOs along the Texas-Mexico Border That Use Mexican Providers

The availability of dual medical systems to both U.S. and Mexican citizens along the border increases border residents' freedom of choice in choosing a physician. In Texas, the vast majority of the border area is designated by the Texas Department of Health as a Health Care Professional Shortage Area, and the area has a lower than average number of hospital beds per resident than the rest of the state. Texas border residents often choose Mexican physicians for reasons of cost, treatment style, and availability.

The border areas of the two nations are bound by cultural and economic ties, and the creation of health maintenance organizations (HMOs) and preferred provider organizations (PPOs) in the United States that include Mexican physicians could lead to greater choice for policyholders and lower physician and hospital costs for insurance companies. With a large common border, cross-border insurance plans can affect the delivery of health care and benefit both patients from the United States and providers in Mexico.

The Texas-Mexico Border Region

The Texas-Mexico border stretches 1,250 miles from the Gulf of Mexico at Brownsville to El Paso. The area comprises more than half of the entire 2,000-mile international boundary with Mexico. There are four Mexican states that border Texas: Chihuahua, Coahuila, Nuevo Leon, and Tamaulipas. With several different definitions of the "border area," the precise definition is not universally agreed upon. The proposed U.S.-Mexico border health commission defines the area to include one hundred kilometers on each side of the border (U.S. Congress, 1993). A General Accounting Office report that studied the availability of medical services in Texas along the Mexican border used a 16-county area to designate the Texas border area (1988, p. 1). The State of Texas itself has differing definitions of the border area. According to the Texas Comptroller of Public Accounts, the border area includes 30 counties, with a total of 56,282 square miles (Border Economic Development Task Force, 1986, p. 14). An Office of the Governor report used a 15-county area when reporting on the health and human service needs along the border (1993, p. 1).

The Texas-Mexico border area is experiencing high population growth rates. Since 1980, Cameron, Hidalgo, and Webb counties have shown growth rates of 24, 35.4, and 34.2 percent respectively (Selwyn, 1993). These percentages represent a much higher growth rate compared to the overall Texas growth rate of 19 percent between 1980 and 1990 (Office of the Governor, 1993, p. 2).

Table 4.1
Population of Texas "Sister Cites" along the Texas Border

Texas City and County	Mexican City and Municipio	Combined Population
Brownsville, Cameron Co.	Matamoros, Matamoros	563,413
McAllen, Hidalgo Co.	Reynosa, Reynosa	666,212
Laredo, Webb Co.	Nuevo Laredo, Nuevo Laredo	352,707
Eagle Pass, Maverick Co.	Piedras Negras, Piedras Negras	134,563
Del Rio, Val Verde Co.	Ciudad Acuña, Acuña	95,057
El Paso, El Paso Co.	Ciudad Juarez, Juarez	1,525,619

Source: Adapted from B. J. Selwyn, *Epidemiological Issues in Family Health along the U.S.-Mexico Border.*

Along the Texas-Mexico border there are six pairs of "sister cities" that have high population densities due to the maquiladoras (see table 4.1). The six sister cities are Brownsville/Matamoros, McAllen/Reynosa, Laredo/Nuevo Laredo, Eagle Pass/Piedras Negras, Del Rio/Ciudad Acuña, and El Paso/Ciudad Juarez.

Table 4.2 shows that the border population is younger, and has a lower per capita income and higher rates of adult and child poverty than the rest of the state. The population is mainly of Hispanic origin, with all but one Texas county, Brewster, having a Hispanic population of 50 percent or higher. Starr County's population is over 97 percent Hispanic (Selwyn, 1993).

Epidemiology in the Border Region

The border area reports a high number of communicable disease cases, many of which are vaccine preventable. Outbreaks of measles are still common in the area. Hispanics have a higher rate of associated deaths from diabetes, and the incidence of diabetes is higher along the border than in the rest of Texas. Older Hispanic women have high cervical cancer rates because of the lack of knowledge for the need for or access to pap screening. Tuberculosis rates are also higher; the border had a rate of 29.8 cases per 100,000 people, while Texas had an overall rate of 14.6. Twenty-two percent of all drug-resistant tuberculosis cases in Texas were reported in this area. Diseases that are rare in the United States, such as Hansen's Disease (leprosy) and rabies, are still found along the border (Office of the Governor, 1993, p. 15).

Table 4.2
Population Demographic Data, Texas Border Counties, 1990 Census

County	Median Age	Per Capita Income	Percent in Poverty	Percent under 18 in Poverty
Brewster	32.4	$10,730	27.6	31.4
Cameron	27.4	$7,125	39.7	50.7
El Paso	27.9	$9,150	26.8	36.1
Hidalgo	26.1	$6,630	41.9	52.7
Hudspeth	27.9	$7,994	38.9	55.1
Jeff Davis	38.6	$9,975	19.7	24.8
Kinney	39.8	$7,931	28.6	40.8
Maverick	25.6	$5,184	50.4	58.3
Presidio	31.5	$6,347	48.1	58.7
Starr	23.9	$4,152	60.0	68.0
Terrell	36.2	$10,146	27.4	38.5
Val Verde	27.8	$7,904	36.4	47.0
Webb	25.5	$6,771	38.2	47.3
Willacy	27.5	$6,074	44.5	57.5
Zapata	29.0	$6,541	41.0	52.6
Total	**27.1**	**$7,657**	**35.8**	**46.3**
State of Texas	**30.8**	**$12,904**	**18.1**	**24.3**

Source: Adapted from Office of the Governor, *Health and Human Service Issues: U.S. (Texas)-Mexico Border.*

Health needs of the area are served by a combination of public, nonprofit, private, local, state, and regional organizations and facilities. Six of the 15 counties have local health departments that served over 190,000 clients in 1990. Three of the eight regions of the Texas Department of Health span the border area. The area also has 20 federally funded community or migrant health centers, which serve indigent populations. Five border counties are also served through the State Primary Care Program, which provides health services through contractors to low-income residents who are not eligible for Medicaid (Office of the Governor, 1993, p. 8).

Seven of the border area counties have no hospital. These counties cover 14,500 square miles and have a total population of 43,000 persons. Five hospitals—in El Paso, Maverick, Starr, Val Verde, and Brewster counties—are owned by hospital districts. A hospital authority operates a public facility in Hidalgo County, but the authority is not obligated to provide indigent care. The entire border area has 9 percent of the Texas population, but only 5 percent of the hospitals and 6 percent of the licensed beds (Office of the Governor, 1993, pp. 9-10). Table 4.3 lists the available hospital facilities and available beds in each of the Texas counties that border Mexico.

Along with the lack of health care facilities in most areas in the region, there is a widespread shortage of health care professionals. Fourteen of the 15 counties are completely or partially designated as Health Care Professional Shortage Areas. The degree of shortage is rated on a scale from one to four, with one being the highest degree of shortage. Five counties are designated as level one in terms of the severity of lack of medical professionals (see table 4.4).

Two counties, Hudspeth and Terrell, have no physician. Overall, there is a 1:984 physician per capita ratio in the border area. The per capita ratio in the United States is 1:411. The border ratio is well below the 1:600 ratio recommend by the World Health Organization (Office of the Governor, 1993, p. 13).

High per capita ratios for other health care professionals further complicate border residents' ability to access health services. In June of 1988, eight of the border counties were designated as dentist shortage areas. The border area has fewer registered and vocational nurses relative to its population as compared to the rest of the state. In 1988, the population to nurse ratio in Texas was 179:1 while the ratio in the border area was 324:1 (General Accounting Office, 1988, pp. 35-36).

The border area is also characterized as having a high percentage of population without any health insurance. Over 35 percent of the border area population is uninsured, versus 18 percent statewide (Office of the Governor, 1993, p. 14). The Lower Rio Grande Valley Primary Health Care Review, which focused on low-income neighborhoods, found that only 47.5 percent of residents of neighborhoods surveyed had health insurance (Selwyn, 1993). Even people with insurance can have trouble finding health care as Medicaid patients often are referred to specialists as far away as Galveston because local professionals will not accept them (Office of the Governor, 1993, p. 14).

Table 4.3
Available Hospitals in Texas along the Mexican Border

County	Public	For Profit	Not for Profit	Total Licensed Beds
Brewster	1	0	0	50
Cameron	1*	2	2	911
El Paso	1	5	1	1,870
Hidalgo	1	2	2	937
Hudspeth	0	0	0	0
Jeff Davis	0	0	0	0
Kinney	0	0	0	0
Maverick	1	0	0	77
Presidio	0	0	0	0
Starr	1	0	0	44
Terrell	0	0	0	0
Val Verde	1	0	0	93
Webb	0	1	1	418
Willacy	0	0	0	0
Zapata	0	0	0	0
Total	7	10	6	4,400

Source: Adapted from Office of the Governor, *Health and Human Service Issues: U.S. (Texas)-Mexico Border.*

*South Texas Hospital is owned by the State of Texas and is required to do some charity care.

Table 4.4
Primary Care Health Professional Shortage Areas

County	Designated HPSA?	Degree of Shortage	Type of Shortage
Brewster	Yes	1*	Partial County
Cameron	Yes	4	Population Group
El Paso	Yes	2	Facility
		1,2	South East, South
Hidalgo	Yes	3	Population Group
Hudspeth	Yes	1	Whole County
Jeff Davis	Yes	2	Whole County w/ Partial County
Kinney	No		
Maverick	Yes	2	Whole County
Presidio	Yes	2	Multiple Parts of County
Starr	Yes	1	Whole County
Terrell	Yes	1	Whole County
Val Verde	Yes	2	Whole County
Webb	Yes	4	Whole County
Willacy	Yes	4	Whole County
Zapata	Yes	3	Whole County

Source: Adapted from Office of the Governor, *Health and Human Service Issues: U.S. (Texas)-Mexico Border*. Austin, Tex., 1993.

* 1 (highest), 4 (lowest).

Use of Medical Services in Mexico by U.S. Residents

Mexico offers border residents an option not available to most U.S. citizens: access to the Mexican medical system. Four studies (see table 4.5) report the percentages of citizens who used medical services in Mexico. Dental care, medical care and medicine purchases were tabulated, and the results showed heavy use of dental services and medicine purchases in Mexico. A Columbus, New Mexico, study demonstrated a bimodal age and ethnic distribution among those using services in Mexico: an older retired Anglo community with a relatively higher per capita income, and a younger Hispanic population with larger families and relatively lower per capita income.

Table 4.5
U.S. Residents' Use of Medical Services in Mexico

Study Location	Medicines	Medical Care	Dental Care
Columbus, New Mexico			
Hispanic	86%	79%	85%
Anglo	46	10	60
Lower Rio Grande Valley, PHCR	28	16	10
Brownsville, Texas	43	44	43
Hidalgo County			
Total	17.1	11.7	24.4
Mexican-American	19.1	13.7	28.3

Sources: Adapted from William McConnell et al., "Cooperation in Health Care across the U.S.-Mexico Border: The Palomas/Columbus Experience"; Lower Rio Grande Valley Development Council, "The Valley Primary Health Care Review: A Report by the Indigent Health Care Council"; Tony Zavaleta et al., "Health Needs Assessment Survey for Brownsville: A U.S.-Mexico Border Community Case Study, 1983-1985"; and William W. Thompson, "Cross-Border Health Care Utilization and Practices of Mexican-Americans in the Lower Rio Grande Valley."

Members of the elderly community are insured by Medicare, but Medicare does not cover the cost of dental care or the cost of medicines. This explains the high use of dental providers and medicine purchases across the border. The Lower Rio Grande Valley Primary Health Care Review and the Health Needs Assessment of the City of Brownsville interviewed citizens in indigent neighborhoods, which may explain the high percentage of use of medical services in Mexico.

The Primary Health Care Review, derived from a model developed by the World Health Organization to evaluate primary health care in nonindustrialized countries, found that 80 percent of the respondents cited cost as the main reason they travel to Mexico for medical services. Data collected by the Families U.S.A. Foundation showed that the costs of six top brand-name prescription drugs purchased in the United States were three times higher, on average, than on the Mexican side of the border (1992, p. 4).

Women from the United States have reported traveling to Mexico to buy less expensive contraceptive pills. A 1979 survey of contraceptive use showed that 10.3 percent of Mexican-American women who used contraceptive pills purchased them in Mexico (Smith, Warren, and Garcia, 1983, p. 70). Some women also reported going to Mexico to be sterilized. In Mexico, women can choose their own private physician and pay less for the procedure (Selwyn et al., 1992, p. 12). In the 1979 study, 4.5 percent of sterilized women reported going to Mexico for the procedure (Smith, Warren, and Garcia, 1983, p. 70). The other common medical purchases documented in a 1993 study include antibiotics, analgesics, and blood pressure medicines (Thompson, 1993, p. 6).

Current Initiatives in Cross-Border Delivery Systems

With the rising costs of employee health care coverage, companies along the U.S.-Mexico border have looked for more cost-efficient ways of providing health care for their workers. Historically, agribusiness has utilized the Mexican system for many years, and now more industries are beginning to look to Mexico as a way to lower costs and give their employees greater choice in health care options. Throughout the United States, traditional indemnity plans are quickly being replaced by health maintenance and preferred provider organizations. With HMOs and PPOs along the border, U.S. companies hope to take advantage of the lower cost of health care in Mexico. At the same time, these plans want to control costs and ensure quality of medical services in Mexico.

Western Growers Association

The agricultural trade group Western Growers Association has provided health benefits in Mexico for 15 years and has operated its own PPO in Mexico for the past 7 years. Of the 70,000 people covered by the association, 10,000 regularly seek care in Mexico. Eighty percent of these people are U.S. residents and the remaining 20 percent are dependents living in Mexico. There is a financial incentive for members to seek care in Mexico. The association pays for 80 percent of the cost of care in the United States after a certain deductible is met. In Mexico, all care is covered after a $2.50 charge per visit is paid. The association estimates that it saves nearly 40 percent on care in Mexico compared with the same care provided in the United States (Fiscus, 1993, p. 1).

Western Growers Association was one of three different companies that developed plans for farmworkers to receive health care in Mexico at the end of 1982. A provider group in the Mexican town of San Luis Colorado, across the river from San Luis, Arizona, offered services at a 43-bed hospital with the latest medical equipment. The company estimated that about 60 percent of their claims were treated in Mexico. Data from one of the major insurance companies showed heavy use of the plan, with a peak of 15,215 claims paid in 1984 (de Zapien et al., 1988).

There are obvious price differences between the medical delivery systems of the United States and Mexico. According to data supplied by one insurance company, the total amount paid for an appendectomy to U.S. providers was $2,705, compared with $1,243.90 to Mexican providers. The insurance company paid out $2,137 for a normal delivery in the United States and $702 for the same procedure in Mexico (de Zapien et al., 1988).

Frontera Health Services

Frontera Health Services acts as a health care provider network mainly serving U.S. companies that employ Mexican residents or whose employees have immediate family members living in Mexico. Frontera has been active in the development of cross-border delivery of health care since 1987. In that year, Frontera entered into a partnership with a Portland-based insurance carrier that specialized in agribusiness coverage and 3 Mexican physicians with experience in health care cost containment. Originally, Frontera had negotiated contracts with eight hospitals and approximately 125 doctors in Tijuana and Mexicali. The doctors agreed to adhere to a set fee schedule and provide discounts on their usual charges in exchange for an expected increase in patient flow. The system was originally established as a means of keeping providers and employees from filing fraudulent or overpriced claims. American insurance companies located far from the border often paid for inflated claims not realizing that health care costs were much lower in Mexico. Also, Mexico did not have checks, review, and cost containment procedures to discourage overbilling for treatment as in the United States (Dower, 1987, p. 13).

Frontera has evolved in the past several years, establishing fully insured programs, whereas in the past it served only self-funded programs. Presently, Frontera has contractual relationships with physicians, hospitals, clinics, and numerous pharmacies in three Mexican cities. Table 4.6 illustrates the available providers at the three locations. (The U.S. cities located across the border from the Mexican cities are listed in italics.) Frontera works with U.S.-based third party administrators to establish and implement a credentialing process for physicians, quality control programs, and a claims review process to facilitate the containment of costs in Mexico. Other important functions that Frontera performs are language and currency conversion on claims and the standardization of transaction codes (Phelps, 1994). According to Paul Schneider, Vice President, the company would like to expand services to Texas once it is firmly established in California (1995).

Table 4.6
Frontera Health Services: Available Medical Facilities

	Tijuana *(San Diego, Calif.)*	Mexicali *(Calxico, Calif.)*	San Luis Rio Colorado *(Yuma, Col.)*
Hospitals	6	1	1
Pharmacies	6	1	2
Primary Care Physicians	7	2	2
Specialists	56	28	26

Source: Paul Schneider, Vice President, E. J. Phelps and Company, telephone interview, March 11, 1995.

According to Jack Phelps, President of Frontera Health Services, there is very little managed care in Mexico besides some utilization review, an analysis of the care provided to individual consumers. Mexican providers are open to managed care concepts, but the education of U.S. providers about Mexican issues is still lacking. Each new company in the U.S. must be informed about quality, cost, and legal issues in Mexico. Frontera will most likely continue to be an innovator in the development of insurance plans in Mexico. Presently, the company is investigating the possibility of developing plans that would allow employees of companies in the U.S. to purchase health coverage for family members in the interior of Mexico (Phelps, 1994).

Servicios Medicos Internacionales

Located in Tijuana and incorporated under Mexican laws, Servicios Medicos Internacionales (SMI) is being marketed as a low-cost health insurance alternative for San Diego businesses that employ a large number of Hispanics. SMI offers services to members for a monthly fee with no copayments, deductibles, or supplemental charges for services. SMI utilizes the services of contract hospitals and doctors, along with staff doctors. All services are treated at SMI-approved facilities, although there is some coverage for life-threatening emergencies at non-SMI facilities (SMI, n.d.).

Upon approval of an application, a member becomes eligible for a wide variety of services, including office or hospital visits, physician and surgeon services, hospital room and board, general nursing and therapy, intensive care, X rays, and preventive services. Limited services include nonchronic drugs, preapproved ambulance services, and maternity care as long as conception was after the plan's effective date. Individual plan costs range from $71 to $111 per month for a single member based on age, with rates for groups slightly cheaper depending on ages and number of members in the group. A dental supplement is available on all plans for an additional $10 per month for individuals (SMI, n.d.).

In San Diego, the Hotel del Coronado's Tijuana-based employees faced a problem when the company switched to a California-based Blue Cross and Blue Shield HMO. Although the employees had authorization to be in the United States and visit the HMO facilities, many of their dependents could not use the services in California. Jerry Ramsdale, the hotel's senior vice president and director of human resources, met with insurance companies and hospital administrators in Tijuana to see what was available in capitated services (i.e., fixed sum of money for each patient assigned to a doctor, independent of how much medical service is needed). He found nothing available but did learn that Servicios Medicos Internacionales was hoping to work with firms for capitated services at a Tijuana facility (CBI, 1994).

Ramsdale worked with SMI and quickly became its first corporate client. The development of this first Mexican HMO won the Hotel del Coronado the Creative Excellence in Benefits award from the Corporate Benefits Institute (CBI, 1994). Since then, the National Steel and Shipbuilding Company and Le Meridien Hotel have signed up as clients (Fikes, 1992, p. 1). Presently, SMI covers approximately 17,000 employees (Fiscus, 1993, p. 27).

Recently, SMI has come under pressure for refusing to pay a claim made by a member who was shot and paralyzed from the waist down during a robbery attempt. Juan Hernandez was a chef at Le Meridien Hotel and operated his own taco shop on the side. Hernandez paid monthly premiums of $168 to SMI for medical coverage and now has medical bills of over $200,000 which SMI refuses to pay. In a letter to Mr. Hernandez's attorney, SMI claimed that Hernandez provided "an incomplete enrollment form" and that, as a business owner, Hernandez should have been covered by workers' compensation. Hernandez's attorney claims that SMI does not request business ownership information on its application. According to Brenda Fagan-Johnson of Westland Insurance Brokers, which handles many SMI policies, the second cause for refusal is a moot point because California does not require workers' compensation for business owners (Rowland, 1994, p. B-1).

The disputed claim highlights the potential problems of working with a Mexican company that operates all services in Mexico. SMI is not licensed by the California Insurance Commission but has a substantial economic interest in California. Fagan-Johnson insists that SMI is responsible for Hernandez's medical costs and states that if the company refuses to pay the claims she will advise her clients to seek other health plans that do not put employees in high-risk situations (Rowland, 1994 p. B-1).

Issues in Cross-Border HMO and PPO Development

Quality of care issues are very important when considering collaborations with medical providers in Mexico. Companies interested in working with Mexican providers need to understand and develop appropriate credentialing standards when choosing providers with whom to contract. With Mexico's unique medical education system and varying hospital quality standards, U.S. provider credentialing requirements cannot be automatically transferred to Mexico. The threat of malpractice and the availability of malpractice insurance in Mexico are an additional concern for a company interested in working with Mexican health care providers.

Hospitals and Medical Schools

Great diversity exists in the facilities and capabilities of hospitals and medical schools in Mexico. This diversity is one of the reasons that there is little standardization or private credentialing among medical facilities and schools. Legislative changes are expected in the near future on the certification of specialties and the accreditation of medical schools (de la Fuente, 1994).

There are 59 medical schools (44 private and 15 public) in Mexico (de la Fuente, 1994). A study published in *American Journal of Public Health* that examined factors contributing to physician under- and unemployment in Mexico classified the nation's medical schools as inadequate, average and good. Although the names and breakdown of the number of schools in each category were not given, the report demonstrates the unevenness in the quality of Mexican medical schools. Limited postgraduate training and education was found to be a contributing factor for physician under- and unemployment. Medical school quality influences the options for postgraduate training, because entrance to a specialty is based on the quality of previous education received (Frenk et al., 1991, p. 25). According to Dr. Juan Ramon de la Fuente, former director of faculty of medicine at the Universidad Autónoma de México and present minister of health, there are only 430 postgraduate residency programs in Mexico, compared to 7,000 residency programs in the United States (1994).

There is a high dropout rate in Mexican medical schools. Mexican students often cannot support themselves financially during their education. Before attaining eligibility for a license to practice medicine in Mexico, a student must complete academic work, clinical training, a predegree internship, social service, and an oral examination. The process usually takes six years to complete. The first two years are spent studying the basic sciences, and the student receives an introduction to clinical work at the end of this period. After completion of the academic training, the student enters a two-year clinical training. During this time the student participates in rotations among internal medicine, surgery, obstetrics, and pediatrics. A one-year predegree rotating internship follows the clinical training component. The final year of medical training consists of the *pasante*, one year of service with the Secretaría de Salud (SSA). These assignments range from prestigious posts in major medical centers to positions as basic health care providers in rural communities. Toward the end of the first six months of the social service component, the student undergoes an oral exam in front of three professors. Upon successful completion of the oral exam, the student is granted a degree. The Ministry of Education records the degree and the Ministry of Health grants the applicant a certification number. Once registered with both organizations, the student is licensed to practice medicine (Warner and Reed, 1993, pp. 84-85).

Malpractice

Mexico has completely different legal and cultural criteria for handling complaints against doctors. Mexican patients with low purchasing power have little recourse if they are dissatisfied with services (Frenk et al., 1994, p. 1,594). According to an administrator at a major hospital in Mexico City, civil malpractice claims are not numerous, but culturally Mexicans are more likely to seek criminal charges against a physician they feel has acted improperly (Hurtado-Belendez, 1994b). Yet Mexican law does provide a legal framework for those people who seek damages against a physician or medical facility. In general, there is little information available about the number of complaints against the medical sector in Mexico. The filing of lawsuits against medical professions is a slowly growing phenomenon in Mexico (FUNSALUD, 1994b, p. 20).

The Mexican law of professions determines which professions require a degree and provides a government registration number. This law also sets the punishment for practicing without the required documents: one to six years in prison and a fine of 100 to 300 times the established minimum daily salary. Besides the general regulation of the profession, the Mexican law of professions states that doctors have certain responsibilities to their patients. If the doctor does not comply with his or her responsibility, there are three possible consequences: the loss of the right to collect charges for medical services, the obligation to pay for damages and harm to the patient, and the conviction of a criminal offense for not following the Mexican law of professions. In the first two instances any complaint would be handled by a civil authority and in the third the matter would be handled by a criminal authority (FUNSALUD, 1994b, pp. 15-16).

Damages are classified into three general categories: material damages, physical damages and moral damages. Different state civil codes determine the legal framework for compensation for damages. The different legal codes do not establish any maximum limit for material damages. In respect to physical damages, the different state laws cannot be set any lower than the federal law of the worker, although in ten states there is no upper limit on physical damage awards. In the federal district, as stated in its civil code, when damages result in death, or partial, total, or permanent disability, the federal law of the worker determines the amount of the award. To calculate an award, the minimum salary of the region is quadrupled and paid for the number of days of the resulting incapacitation. For example, if the patient dies, the indemnity would be the equivalent of 790 days of minimum salary, which is N$11,632.75 (approximately $3,580) at 1994 salary levels. For a total or partial incapacity that lasts for an undetermined period, the amount would equal 1,095 days of minimum salary. The maximum amounts for moral damages vary widely throughout the states, with no limits in Puebla and Sonora, and a N$50 limit in Jalisco (FUNSALUD, 1994b, p. 18).

Seguros de Responsabilidad Civil (Civil Responsibility Insurance)

In Mexico, there currently exists a type of malpractice insurance that guarantees payment for damages resulting from negligence or incompetence in the exercise of the medical attention. In general, there are two types of insurance. The first covers doctors practicing anywhere in Mexico and the doctor employees while they are working in an official capacity. The second type of insurance covers hospitals and clinics. In Mexico, there are only 40 insurance companies that offer this type of insurance. According to the insurance companies there are only 707 current policies for doctors. The annual premiums range between N$900 and N$3,500 according to the amount insured. Only 30 hospital units have this insurance. According to 1992 figures on the number of doctors and hospital units, only 0.72 percent of doctors and 0.21 percent of hospitals are insured (FUNSALUD, 1994b, p. 20). Although coverage has been limited in the past, large hospitals and physician office buildings are now starting to require practicing physicians to have this insurance to protect the prestige of their institution (Hurtado-Belendez, 1994b).

Case Study: Laredo, Texas, and Nuevo Laredo, Tamaulipas

During a recent visit to Laredo and Nuevo Laredo, I had the opportunity to speak with private and public physicians, public health officials, and hospital administrators about the current availability of medical services in both areas, cross-border utilization of medical services, and the possibility of increased interaction between insurance companies in the United States and medical providers in Mexico. Although this visit was not a scientific study of conditions in the area, the visit did lead to a better understanding of the obstacles and advantages of establishing HMOs or PPOs along the U.S.-Mexico border that include the participation of Mexican medical providers.

The twin cities of Laredo and Nuevo Laredo face many of the same problems mentioned earlier. The population of Laredo is 133,239, according to the 1990 census. The population is relatively young, low income, and Hispanic. Located in Webb County, the vital statistics for Laredo and the entire county show tuberculosis rates that are almost three times the national average and twice the state average. There is also a high incidence and prevalence of hepatitis, gastrointestinal and skin ailments, and immunization-preventable diseases. The area has a scarcity of health care resources and high patient to health care provider ratios (City of Laredo Health Department, 1994, pp. 19-20).

Nuevo Laredo had an official population of 219,468 in 1990 and has seen a population growth rate of 8 percent since 1980. The median age in Nuevo Laredo is 22.1. Seventy-five percent of residents ages 15 and older have completed primary school. Ninety percent of the population of Nuevo Laredo is adequately immunized (Selwyn, 1993).

There are three private hospitals and 15 clinics located in Laredo. The major facility in the area is Mercy Regional Medical Center, with 288 beds and a recently completed coronary care unit. The area also has Doctor's Hospital, with 95 beds and a 64-bed psychiatric and substance abuse hospital (Laredo Chamber of Commerce, 1990, p. 12). The City of Laredo Health Department offers tuberculosis services, WIC administration, dental care, and HIV-AIDS services. The Gateway Community Health Center provides care to the local medically indigent population.

Nuevo Laredo offers a mix of both public and private hospitals and medical providers. Of nine medical centers, four are public entities. The largest private entity, Hospital San José, has 140 beds; the smallest, Hospital de Especialidades, has 19 beds (Carrizales, 1991).

Laredo residents make substantial use of medical services in Nuevo Laredo. City of Laredo employee health insurance covers health care obtained in Nuevo Laredo (Antú, 1994). People often cross the border for the treatment of other diseases, such as sexually transmitted diseases, because treatment is cheaper, faster, and more confidential than in Laredo (Robinson, 1994). Facilities in Nuevo Laredo are open nights and weekends, which make them more convenient to visit. In Laredo, patients often have to wait for an appointment, in some cases up to one month for an obstetrician/gynecologist appointment, which makes a provider in Nuevo Laredo more attractive (Baber, 1994). The treatment style of Mexican physicians also attracts patients from the United States (Cardenas, 1994).

Currently, certain medical providers in Nuevo Laredo are actively trying to attract patients from the United States through advertising in Laredo newspapers and on billboards at border crossings. One hospital, Hospital de Especialidades, considers itself to be in direct competition with hospitals in Laredo. The medical director, Dr. Eudimio Cardenas, believes that the hospital can offer substantial savings and would like to work with U.S. insurance companies (1994). The five-year-old hospital has 6 general doctors and 60 specialists.

Hospital de Especialidades is currently processing claims with Blue Cross and Blue Shield of Texas and Mutual of Omaha. All claims for Blue Cross and Blue Shield of Texas have to be preapproved. Carolina Sánchez, who handles the claims for the hospital, estimated that she is currently submitting four to five claims a month to U.S. insurance companies. According to Sánchez, the checks go directly to the patient and the patient pays the hospital. There have been no claims rejected by insurance companies, but many claims are pending, with processing times lasting two to four months (1994). There are standardized costs for surgery and hospital rooms but not for doctor services. All claims sent to insurance companies must be completed in English with prices stated in dollars.

Attempts to control costs have been a major concern for insurance companies in the United States. With only a small percentage of the Mexican population covered by private health insurance, the concept of managed care is almost nonexistent in Mexico. Although the concept is not widely understood from the insurance perspective, there have been informal cost controls practiced by physicians along the border. Mexican physicians have never had the opportunity to recover from insurance companies the cost of services provided. Border providers have always had to consider the cost of treatment because patients pay out of pocket. Providers are therefore careful about the type of care and often discuss treatment charges with patients. Informal cost control makes it necessary for doctors to diagnose problems without detailed tests or expensive equipment (Antú, 1994). Without fear of lawsuits, doctors are able to treat patients more economically by not practicing defensive medicine (Cardenas, 1994).

Attempts to control costs have also led insurance companies to be more selective in choosing providers and to establish protocols for certain treatments. Dr. Cardenas reported that he would be more than willing—and he believed most doctors in the border region would be willing—to follow a payment schedule adopted by an insurance company. Dr. Cardenas felt that the lack of an agreement between his hospital and the insurance companies was a major problem, and he welcomed a visit from insurance companies and businesses looking for more economical alternatives for their employees' health care (1994). One insurance claims processor also expressed interest in having insurance representatives from the United States visit to explain the process for filing claims (Sánchez, 1994).

The health authority for the City of Laredo health department, Dr. L. F. Mendoza, who also works in the private sector in Laredo, identified several of the problem areas in establishing binational health insurance plans. He said the idea was interesting and he considered including dentists in Mexico when recently establishing a third party administrator for a local business. No Mexican providers were eventually included in the plan. Dr. Mendoza's first concern was how doctors would be credentialed and compensated for their services. He also had a concern that there would be little control over inflated prices or charges for services not rendered. Another of his concerns was the lack of standardized medical recordkeeping in Mexico. He also pointed out that any threat of malpractice would inevitably focus on the U.S. side of the border, as complainants look to the "deep pockets" of large U.S. corporations (1994).

Conclusion

NAFTA has focused greater attention on the U.S.-Mexico border area; the lack of access to medical care has been well documented throughout the region. The use of medical services in Mexico is not the definitive answer for increasing access to health care, but could play an important role in developing new alternatives for a medically underserved area. The Texas-Mexico border area, with its high rates of poverty and low number of health care providers could benefit from the availability of Mexican medical providers. U.S. residents have traveled to Mexico for medical care in the past and U.S. insurance companies could develop insurance products to facilitate policyholder access to Mexican providers. Companies in other border states are currently developing insurance plans that include Mexican providers.

Any successful venture into the Mexican medical market will require an understanding of the prevailing market forces in both the United States and Mexico, along with a basic knowledge of Mexico's private and public system. Any company interested in developing cross-border plans needs to be familiar with issues of doctor and hospital credentialing, quality of care, and malpractice issues. Substantial risk is involved in developing a venture with providers from another country, but cooperation has existed for several years. It is possible that U.S. employers or insurance companies could be a target for lawsuits, but risks exist in any managed care plan, regardless of its location (Reavey, 1993, p. 5).

Chapter 5. Exploratory Survey of Health Insurance Companies Licensed to Sell in Texas, Current and Planned Collaborative Ventures in the Mexico Market

With the continued concern over rising health care costs accompanied by the growing number of uninsured individuals, cooperation between health providers and consumers in the border states and Mexico is increasingly attractive. Individuals have crossed the border in search of medical services in the past and will continue do so to as a means of locating affordable, culturally appropriate health care. This survey assesses post-NAFTA interactions between medical providers and consumers in Texas and Mexico.

Cross-border medical issues will affect the Texas medical insurance industry, the Texas Department of Insurance, federal and state government, and consumers. The State of Texas, with its proximity to Mexico, can lead the way to increased and more creative cooperation between health care providers, consumers, and third party payers. State insurance departments have played a vital role in past and current efforts to address problems with the cost and availability of health insurance. The Texas Department of Insurance, by sponsoring this exploratory survey, has positioned itself to provide preliminary information about such collaborations to interested corporate clients and consumers.

Survey Design

A survey instrument was developed to explore cooperative relationships between patients, providers, and third-party payers in Texas and Mexico. The first part of the survey assesses the extent of coverage offered to U.S. citizens who, by necessity or choice, access medical care in Mexico. Respondents were asked about the types of care covered by policies including emergency care, specialty care, and primary care in Mexico. Respondents were also asked whether their companies have formed any agreements with Mexican doctors or hospitals for treatment of U.S. nationals in Mexico.

The survey inquired about coverage of Mexican nationals for treatment in the United States and the participation of Mexican providers in Texas HMOs and PPOs. Companies were also asked about their plans for expanding services along the border and into the interior of Mexico. Finally, the U.S.-based insurers were asked to assess their knowledge of the implications of NAFTA on their own industry's ability to enter the Mexican health insurance market.

All companies surveyed were licensed to sell accident and health insurance in Texas as of December 31, 1993. A total of 538 surveys were sent out under the auspices of the Texas Department of Insurance (see the appendix). The survey did not apply to all 538 companies because companies that sold health insurance were not able to be isolated from the entire group prior to the mailing. The companies that received the survey may sell one or a combination of individual and group life insurance, disability insurance, Medicare supplements, or major medical policies. Many companies wrote on the returned survey that they sold no major medical insurance. Unless explicitly stated, there is no way to distinguish between companies that do not sell major medical policies and those that sell major medical policies with no coverage component in Mexico. Although this is a weakness, the survey contains important information about the interaction of Texas insurance companies with Mexican providers.

All companies were asked to indicate on their responses if they wanted their individual company results to remain confidential. Companies were asked to choose between keeping all answers confidential, permitting all answers to be released, and requesting that answers to specific questions remain confidential.

Of the 107 companies reporting some coverage in Mexico, 86 percent requested that their responses remain confidential. All of the HMOs responding chose to have their answers remain confidential.

Survey Findings: Coverage by U.S. Insurance Companies

A total of 404 companies responded to the survey, which represents a response rate of over 75 percent. Of the responding organizations, 107 stated that they sold health insurance that provided some coverage for services in Mexico. Eleven HMOs reported providing some form of coverage in Mexico.

The results of the survey responses on care covered in Mexico are tabulated in table 5.1. Of the responding companies, most companies covered only emergency care in Mexico. Forty-five companies reported that over 75 percent of their policies included emergency coverage in Mexico.

A total of 37 companies answered they covered primary and/or specialty care for insureds near the Mexico border allowing them to seek care in Mexico.

Eight companies reported writing policies for Mexican nationals for care in the United States. One company reported selling indemnity products in the United States near the Mexican border that have the same rates as those sold to U.S. residents.

Forty-four companies replied that they provided both emergency and primary/specialty care in Mexico. One company responded that they provided this coverage by default because their policies pay for coverage anywhere in the world, but they "do not seek this business." Similarly, another company stated they answered the survey questions affirmatively "only because our polices do not limit coverage to the U.S."

Fifty-three companies responded that they supplied coverage for U.S. residents traveling to Mexico for a specific period of time. Several companies limited coverage to "provide

Table 5.1
Health Insurance Companies in Texas That Cover U.S. Insureds in Mexico

Polices That Cover Care in Mexico (in percent)	**Group**	**Individual**	**Both**	**Not Stated**
Emergency Care				
<25	1	7	0	1
25-50	0	2	0	1
51-75	0	1	0	0
>76	27	13	13	2
Not Stated	3	4	7	5
Primary/Specialty Care				
<25	1	2	0	0
25-50	0	1	0	0
51-75	0	1	0	0
>76	10	10	3	0
Not Stated	2	2	3	3
Emergency and Primary/Specialty Care				
<25	1	2	0	0
25-50	0	0	0	0
51-75	0	1	0	0
>76	12	9	7	0
Not Stated	4	2	3	3
U.S. Residents Who Travel to Mexico				
<25	5	2	0	0
25-50	1	2	0	0
51-75	0	0	0	0
>76	14	9	6	0
Not Stated	4	1	5	4

Source: Request for information pursuant to Texas Insurance Code Article 1.24; *Current and Projected Activities in the Mexican Market and with Mexican Health Care Providers*, Texas Department of Insurance.

coverage, care, or treatment of sudden onset of serious illness or injury while traveling on business or pleasure, not to exceed 90 days of such care or treatment." Another company stated that they covered insureds when traveling abroad on business or pleasure so long as they are not out of the country for more than 90 consecutive days.

Of all the companies that reported providing coverage in Mexico, only one company stated they had any agreement with a Mexican hospital or doctor. This implies that, although care may not be specifically excluded from coverage, few companies encourage insureds to use Mexican hospitals or doctors, unlike companies in California that are experimenting with HMOs and PPOs that utilize Mexican providers (see chapter 5). Although no HMO or PPO indicated that they included Mexican providers practicing in Mexico for members who live near the Texas-Mexico border, two companies responded that any services in Mexico would be reimbursed at network benefit rates.

Expansion into Mexico

U.S. companies indicated some interest in expanding into the Mexican market. This appears to be a niche market, of interest to a limited number of companies. Table 5.2 lists the number of companies and their expressed interest in various aspects of expanding into Mexico. Six companies stated that they were interested in including Mexican providers in their insurance plans.

Table 5.2
Number of Companies Planning to Expand Services in Mexico

Type of Participation	Companies
Joint venture with Mexican company	5
Increased sales of policies to Mexican nationals	4
Administrative functions for claims in the United States	2
Aid in the creation of managed care in Mexico	6
Aid in the negotiation of discounts for medical services in the U.S.	2
Aid in the development of doctor and hospital credentialing	1
Inclusion of Mexican physicians and hospitals for approved services	6
Other	0

Source: Request for information pursuant to Texas Insurance Code Article 1.24; *Current and Projected Activities in the Mexican Market and with Mexican Health Care Providers*, Texas Department of Insurance.

Table 5.3 shows the perceived barriers to the inclusion of Mexican physicians and hospitals in current insurance plans. Insurance companies were asked to mark all of the listed conditions that they considered barriers to including Mexican providers in an HMO or PPO. Accreditation of Mexican physicians and hospitals was most often cited as a perceived barrier. Language and cultural issues were also cited as barriers by those companies answering the question. A high number of companies chose not to answer this question. This could indicate a lack of interest in or knowledge of the Mexican health care delivery system.

The perceived barriers to participation in the Mexican insurance industry are listed in Table 5.4. Companies marked all of the listed conditions they believed were barriers to active participation in the Mexican insurance industry. Unfamiliarity with the medical delivery system in Mexico was most often cited as a barrier to entry into the market. The uncertainty of the market was also cited by many companies. Fewer companies chose not to answer the question, compared with the previous question on the use of Mexican providers near the Texas border.

Table 5.3
Perceived Barriers by Insurance Companies to the Inclusion of Mexican Physicians and Hospitals along the Border
(Number of Companies)

Perceived Barrier	Companies
Accreditation of physicians	47
Accreditation of hospitals	46
Acceptance of managed care by Mexican physicians	35
Malpractice issues	31
Language/cultural issues	40
Lack of potential profit	23
Other	16
No response	41

Source: Request for information pursuant to Texas Insurance Code Article 1.24; *Current and Projected Activities in the Mexican Market and with Mexican Health Care Providers*, Texas Department of Insurance.

Table 5.4
Perceived Barriers by Insurers to Participation in the Mexican Insurance Market (Number of Companies)

Perceived Barrier	Companies
Government regulation	40
Uncertain markets	50
Political instability	41
Limited insurance infrastructure	29
Unfamiliarity with medical delivery system and insurance in Mexico	57
Other	16
No response	30

Source: Request for information pursuant to Texas Insurance Code Article 1.24; *Current and Projected Activities in the Mexican Market and with Mexican Health Care Providers*, Texas Department of Insurance.

Table 5.5 and table 5.6 list responses for the self-assessed knowledge of insurance provisions of NAFTA and their implications for U.S. companies entering the Mexican market. Companies were asked to rate their knowledge on these topics on a scale from one to five, with one being very familiar and five being not familiar. Responses indicated limited knowledge of either topic.

Table 5.5
Familiarity of Insurance Companies with Insurance Provisions of NAFTA

	Very Familiar	Familiar	Somewhat Familiar	A Little Familiar	Not At All Familiar
# of Responses	1	4	19	25	57

Source: Request for information pursuant to Texas Insurance Code Article 1.24; *Current and Projected Activities in the Mexican Market and with Mexican Health Care Providers*, Texas Department of Insurance.

Table 5.6
Familiarity of Insurance Companies with U.S. Companies' Entrance into the Mexican Insurance Market

	Very Familiar	Familiar	Somewhat Familiar	A Little Familiar	Not At All Familiar
# of Responses	0	5	16	28	58

Source: Request for information pursuant to Texas Insurance Code Article 1.24; *Current and Projected Activities in the Mexican Market and with Mexican Health Care Providers*, Texas Department of Insurance.

Conclusion

Presently, many health insurance companies provide health care coverage in Mexico. Although the majority of companies indicated that only emergency care was covered in Mexico, several companies cover all care in Mexico. While comprehensive health care coverage for U.S. nationals in Mexico may not be widely available at this time, it is an option worth exploring by those living and conducting business in the border area. Insurance companies that are actively insuring individuals in this area should investigate the possibility of establishing cooperative agreements with Mexican providers.

The insurance industry in Texas has the potential to form a cooperative relationship with the Mexican health care system. Texas insurance companies have made limited attempts to contract with Mexican providers. By developing more cooperative relations with Mexican providers, Texas insurance companies can help control health care costs and give customers greater freedom of choice in choosing providers. If companies begin to explore this area, it could be the basis for a long-term and collaborative relationship between insurance companies and health providers in Mexico.

The survey results suggest there are substantial barriers to developing agreements with Mexican providers, but some interest exists in exploring this option. The responses to the perceived barriers express the apprehension of U.S. companies and indicate a need for increasing familiarity with the Mexican medical system.

Chapter 6. Conclusion

In general, U.S. insurers are not stampeding across the border to expand their health insurance services in Mexico. However, the companies that have entered, or are exploring increased interaction with Mexico, will make a significant impact on the health insurance industry in Mexico and health care access along the U.S.-Mexico border. Organizations interested in investing in the Mexican health insurance industry will be better prepared to make informed investment decisions by examining the companies active in the Mexican market and exploring the environment in which they operate.

Collaboration between U.S. and Mexican insurance industries is likely to be more fruitful when projects capitalize on the strengths of each system. Both the Mexican health care delivery system and health insurance industry will benefit from the maturity and experience of the U.S. system. An experienced, U.S.-based insurer could use its experience and knowledge to help Mexican insurance companies adapt to a rapidly changing health care delivery environment. Although this investment is not without its risks and obstacles, a realistic strategy is likely to result in a positive experience.

Any direct investment in a Mexican insurance company must be considered over the long term. Although the current social security system may change in the future, companies cannot expect radical change overnight. Yet, any company that has established itself in the Mexican market by demonstrating superior performance and innovation within the limited insurance infrastructure will be positioned for significant rewards when reforms in social security eventually occur.

Access to Mexican doctors and hospitals offers a unique opportunity for insurance companies active along the U.S.-Mexico border. Acknowledging the existing obstacles in the development of a cross-border HMO or PPO, companies interested in the border area should develop and maintain close relations with Mexican doctors and hospitals. Developing cross-border insurance plans could not only offer new products but also provide the necessary experience to facilitate direct investment in the Mexican insurance industry. As the market matures, there will be new investment opportunities for U.S. companies. After the year 2000, U.S.-based companies will be able to enter the market without a Mexican partner.

Recommendations

1. Health insurance companies interested in investing in Mexican insurance companies should investigate and understand the history and current conditions of the Mexican national health system. Yet it is not sufficient to understand the role of the public and private sectors. Interested companies should use all available resources to understand the different cultural aspects of health care delivery in

Mexico. Just as the medical systems are radically different in the United States and Mexico, the attitudes toward health insurance and medical care are different as well. The unique relationship between doctor and patient will affect all aspects of implementing new insurance procedures and policies.

2. The possibility of including Mexican providers in cross-border insurance schemes should be explored by Texas insurance companies. With these collaborative opportunities, the possibility of expanding cost-effective coverage to an underinsured population is a realistic one. By investigating current cross-border insurance activity in California and taking advantage of academic research, Texas companies can build upon the experience of other successful collaborations and adapt them for the Texas-Mexico border area. Physicians who received their basic medical training in Mexico and are currently practicing in the United States could help inform companies exploring the possibilities of working with Mexican providers (Antú, 1994). The only way to succeed in the field is to develop and maintain close working relationships with Mexican physicians and hospitals.

Appendix. Texas Department of Insurance Survey: Current and Planned Activities of Texas Health Insurers in the Mexican Market

1. Do any of the policies your company writes provide the following coverages? Please provide your answers in the table below:

1a. Emergency coverage for insureds traveling in Mexico?

1b. Coverage of primary or specialty care for insureds near the Mexico border allowing them to seek care in Mexico?

1c. Coverage for both emergency and primary/specialty care in Mexico?

1d. Coverage for U.S. residents who travel to Mexico for a specific period of time? (For example, U.S. retirees living in Mexico for part of the year, employees of American companies working in Mexico.)

Question	Yes/No	Group, Individual, Both	Percent of Total Policies with This Coverage
1a			
1b			
1c			
1d			

2. For products that include coverage in Mexico, do you have agreements with any Mexican doctors or hospitals? (Please circle yes or no.)

YES NO

2a. If the answer to 2 is yes, please mark the advantages for you or your insureds.

__ Direct payment by insurance companies to doctors or hospitals

__ Reduced or eliminated coinsurance or deductible

__ Higher percentage of total payment made by insurance company

__ Other (please specify)

3. If you have agreements with Mexican physicians or hospitals, what accreditation requirements have you established? (Please answer on a separate sheet of paper if you prefer.)

4. If you have agreements with Mexican physicians or hospitals, have you also established translation services for these individuals or organizations?

5. Are you writing policies for Mexican nationals for care in the United States? (Please answer on a separate piece of paper if you prefer.)

YES NO

5a. Where are they sold?

5b. What services are covered?

5c. How do rates compare with those sold in the United States?

Questions 6 and 7 are for HMOs and PPOs only

6. Do your services currently include Mexican providers practicing in Mexico for members who live near the Texas-Mexico border?

6a. Cities where coverage is available

6b. Number of members

6c. Group or individual

6d. Number of participating Mexican physicians and hospitals

6e. Are reimbursement rates different than those for doctors and hospitals in the United States? (Please explain.)

7. If you answered yes to question 6, please mark the types of care provided in Mexico.

__ Preventive

__ Specialty care

__ Prenatal/well baby

__ Alternative

__ Emergency

__ Other (please specify)

Questions 8-12 are for all companies

8. Are there any plans to expand services to Mexico? Please mark all applicable activities and provide necessary information.

__ Joint venture with Mexican insurance company

__ Increased sales of policies to Mexican nationals

__ Administrative functions for claims in the United States

__ Aid in the creation of managed care in Mexico

__ Aid in the negotiation of discounts for medical services in the United States

__ Aid in the development of hospital and doctor credentialing

__ Inclusion of Mexican physicians and hospitals for approved services

__ Other (please explain)

9. Please mark all of the perceived barriers to the inclusion in insurance plans of Mexican physicians and hospitals along the border. If possible, please elaborate on why these are barriers.

__ Accreditation of physicians

__ Accreditation of hospitals

__ Acceptance of managed care by Mexican physicians

__ Malpractice issues

__ Language/cultural issues

__ Lack of potential profit

__ Other (please state)

10. Please mark all of the perceived barriers to U.S. insurance companies' active participation in the Mexican insurance industry. If possible, please elaborate on why these are barriers.

__ Government regulation

__ Uncertain markets

__ Political instability

__ Limited insurance infrastructure

__ Unfamiliarity with medical delivery system and insurance in Mexico

__ Other (please specify)

11. On the scale of one (very familiar) to five (not at all familiar) what is your familiarity with the provisions of the North American Free Trade Agreement (NAFTA) regarding insurance?

Very familiar 1 2 3 4 5 not familiar

11. On the scale of one (very familiar) to five (not at all familiar) what is your familiarity of current efforts of U.S. insurance companies' entrance into Mexican insurance market?

Very familiar 1 2 3 4 5 not familiar

References

Aguilar, Concepción. 1994. Director of Actuarial Services, Benefact Actuarios Consultores, S.A. de C.V., Mexico City. Interview, July 21.

Antú, Jose. 1994. Director, Buenavida Health Education Program, City of Laredo Health Department, Laredo, Tex. Interview, December 7-8.

Armenta, Dolores. 1994. Asociación Mexicana de Instituciones de Seguros, Gerente de Seguros de Personas, Mexico City. Interview, July 28.

Asociación Mexicana de Instituciones de Seguros (AMIS). 1993a. *El Seguro Mexicano.* Mexico City, Mexico.

———. 1993b. *Estadística de Primas y Siniestros Directos Acumulados (Cuarto Trimestre).* Mexico City. Mexico.

Baber, Laura. 1994. Coordinator/Clinician, Los Dos Laredos Tuberculosis Elimination Binational Project, Laredo, Tex. Interview, December 8.

Bennett, Russell A. 1994. "Desirable Types of Projects and Joint Venture Projects." Paper presented at a conference on "Health Care in Mexico: Infrastructure, Technologies and Financing: Challenges and Opportunities." La Jolla, Calif. (July 18).

Border Economic Development Task Force. 1986. *Border Economic Development Task Force: Final Report and Recommendations.* Austin, Tex. (December.)

Cameron County Primary Health Care Review Committee. 1991. *Cameron County Primary Health Care Review.* Report. Cameron County Government and the Lower Rio Grande Valley Development Council, The University of Texas Health Science Center at Houston School of Public Health: Houston, Tex. (October.)

Cardenas, Eudimio. 1994. Medical Director, Hospital de Especialidades, Nuevo Laredo, Tamaulipas. Interview, December 8.

Carrizales, Norma. 1991. "Estudio de la Comunidad: Presentado por la Pasante de Enfermeria." Nuevo Laredo, Tamaulipas. (Student paper.)

City of Laredo Health Department. 1994. Health risk factors need assessment. Federal grant application (June 30).

Comisión Nacional de Seguros y Fianzas (CNSF). 1994. *Ley de Instituciones de Sociedades Mutualistas de Seguros.* Mexico City, Mexico.

———. 1995. *The Mexican Insurance Sector.* Mexico City. (Promotional material.)

Comisión Nacional de Seguros y Fianzas and Asociación Mexican de Instituciones de Seguros. 1993. *Sistema Estadístico del Sector Aseguradora.* Mexico City: Comisión Nacional de Seguros y Fianzas. (September 13.)

Coronado, Luis. 1994. "Role of HMOs in the Domestic Market." Paper presented at a conference on "Health Care in Mexico: Infrastructure, Technologies, and Financing: Challenges and Opportunities." La Jolla, Calif. (July 18.)

Corporate Benefits Institute (CBI). 1994. *The Creative Excellence in Benefits Award.* (Promotional material.)

Deener, Bill. 1994. "Treating a Need: Dallas Firm on Leading Edge of Building Hospitals in Mexico." *Dallas Morning News* (November 22).

de la Fuente, Juan Ramon. 1994. "Training, Education, and Accreditation: The Requirements of the Next Generation of Mexican Physicians." Paper presented at a conference on "Health Care in Mexico: Infrastructure, Technologies and Financing: Challenges and Opportunities." La Jolla, Calif. (July 19).

DePalma, Anthony. 1995. "Turmoil Grips Mexico City over Shock Plan for Economy." *International Herald Tribune* (March 13).

de Zapien, Jill Guernsey, et al. 1988. "Where Have All the Farmworkers Gone?: Dynamics of Health Care along the U.S.-Mexico Border." Tuscon: University of Arizona College of Medicine.

Diario Oficial. 1994. Mexico, D.F.: Secretaría de Gobernación. (May 27.)

Dower, Rick. 1987. "Phelps Starts Mexican PPO for U.S. Firms." *San Diego Business Journal* (August 3).

Dykewicz, Paul. 1993. "Insurers Put a Premium on Mexican Market." *Journal of Commerce and Commercial,* vol. 397, no. 28015 (July 9).

"El Diagnóstico Reconoce Debilidades: Es Necesaria la Reforma del IMSS: Genaro Borrego." 1995. *Epoca* (April 3).

Families U.S.A. Foundation. 1992. *Going to Mexico: Priced out of American Health Care.* Washington, D.C. (November.)

Fikes, Bradley J. 1992. "Three San Diego Firms Join HMO Based in Tijuana." *San Diego Business Journal,* vol. 13, no. 41 (October 12).

Fiscus, James W. 1993. "Border Crossing: Some U.S. Businesses Have Found It Profitable to Use Mexican MCOs." *Managed Healthcare News,* vol. 3, no. 5 (May).

Frenk, Julio. 1994a. Comments made at a conference on "Health Care in Mexico: Infrastructure, Technologies, and Financing: Challenges and Opportunities." La Jolla, Calif. (July 18-19).

———. 1994b. "Healthcare in Transition: Innovations in Healthcare Systems: An International Perspective." Paper presented at a conference on "Health Care in Mexico: Infrastructure, Technologies, and Financing: Challenges and Opportunities." La Jolla, Calif. (July 19).

———. 1995. Director, Fundación Mexicana para la Salud, Mexico City. Interview, January 11.

Frenk, Julio, et al. 1991. "Patterns of Medical Employment: A Survey of Imbalances in Urban Mexico." *American Journal of Public Health*, vol. 81, no. 1 (January).

———. 1994. "Consequences of the North American Free Trade Agreement for the Health Services: A Perspective from Mexico." *American Journal of Public Health*, vol. 84, no. 10 (October).

Fundación Mexicana para la Salud (FUNSALUD). 1994a. *Economía y Salud: Propuestas para el Avance del Sistema de Salud en México, Informe Final.* Mexico City.

———. 1994b. *La Protección del Consumidor en el Campo de la Salud.* Mexico City.

General Accounting Office. 1988. *Health Care: Availability in the Texas-Mexico Border Area.* HRD-89-12. Washington, D.C.: Government Printing Office.

Goe, Steven. 1995. Vice President International Markets, ScrippsHealth, La Jolla, Calif. Telephone interview, July 10.

Grupo Nacional Provincial. 1994. *Tarifas Gastos Medicos.* Mexico City.

Hatcher, Jeanette, Jillian Hopewell, Adriana Guardiola, Kathy Jacquart, Walter Moreau, Jeff Stys, Louis DeNino, and David Warner. 1995. *The Border Health Authority: Issues and Design.* U.S.-Mexican Policy Studies Program, Occasional Paper no. 6. Austin, Tex.: Lyndon B. Johnson School of Public Affairs.

Hernandez, Luis. 1994. "Non-Profit Hospitals in Mexico: Different Needs, Different Problems." Paper presented at a conference on "Health Care in Mexico: Infrastructure, Technologies, and Financing: Challenges and Opportunities." La Jolla, Calif. (July 18).

Hinojosa, Magda. 1995. International Service, Baylor Hospital, Dallas Tex. Telephone interview, March 22.

Hurtado-Belendez, Antonio. 1994a. "Achieving Accreditation for New Hospitals: Current Requirements." Paper presented at a conference on "Health Care in Mexico: Infrastructure, Technologies, and Financing: Challenges and Opportunities." La Jolla, Calif. (July 18).

———. 1994b. Vice President, Hospital Angeles de Pedegral. Mexico City. Interview, July 22.

International Medical Associates, Inc. 1994. "Opportunities for U.S. Participation in the Expansion of the Mexican Health Care System." Project identification mission prepared for the U.S. Trade and Development Agency. La Jolla, Calif. (July 18).

Laredo Chamber of Commerce. 1990. *Los Dos Laredos*. Laredo, Tex.

Laurell, Cristina, and Maria Ortega. 1992. "The Free Trade Agreement and Health Services." *International Journal of Health Services*, vol. 22, no. 2.

Lista de Mexico. 1993. *Trato de Libre Comercio, Anexo VII*. Mexico City.

Lower Rio Grande Valley Development Council. 1989. *The Valley Primary Health Care Review: A Report by the Indigent Health Care Council*. Houston, Tex.: The University of Texas Health Science Center.

McConnell, William, et al. 1989. "Cooperation in Health Care across the U.S.-Mexico Border: The Palomas/Columbus Experience." *Border Health,* vol. 5, no. 1 (January).

Martinez-Banuet, Rogelio. 1994. Cardioloist, Mexico City. Interview, July 23.

Meagher, Lawrence. 1995a. President and Chief Executive Officer, The International Hospital Corporation, Dallas, Tex. Interview, April 13.

———. 1995b. President and Chief Executive Officer, International Hospital Corporation, Dallas, Tex. Telephone interview, May 22.

Mendoza, L. F. 1994. Health Authority, City of Laredo Health Department, Laredo, Tex. Interview, December 7.

Miller, Henry. 1993. "Health Care and Insurance in Mexico." *International Section News* (June).

Moreno, Martin, and Noe Cruz. 1995. "De Como el Seguro Social Llego al Caos." *Epoca* (April 3).

Moss, Kendal. 1992. "Improving Patient Transfers across the U.S. Mexico Border." Professional Report, Lyndon B. Johnson School of Public Affairs, The University of Texas at Austin.

"NAFTA Effects." 1993. *Austin Insurance Reports*, vol. 36, no. 48. (September 23.)

National Academy of Medicine, Mexico. 1993. *The North American Free Trade Agreement and Medical Services: Elements for Analysis and Negotiation.* Mexico, D.F.

Nichols, Andrew W., et al. 1991. *Utilization of Health Services along the U.S.-Mexico Border.* Monograph no. 23. Southwest Border Rural Health Research Center, University of Arizona, College of Medicine, Tucson, Ariz. (April).

Nunez, Jose. 1995. Head of International Relations, Methodist Hospital, Houston, Tex. Telephone interview, March 24.

Office of the Governor. 1993. *Health and Human Service Issues: U.S. (Texas)-Mexico Border.* Austin, Tex.

Phelps, Jack. 1994. "Status of HMO Development and Demand: The U.S. Model and Application to Mexico." Paper presented at a conference on "Health Care in Mexico: Infrastructure, Technologies, and Financing: Challenges and Opportunities." La Jolla, Calif. (July 18).

Ramírez de Alba, Juan. 1994. "Demographic and Economics of the Market for Health Care Products and Technologies." Paper presented at a conference on "Health Care in Mexico: Infrastructure, Technologies, and Financing: Challenges and Opportunities." La Jolla, Calif. (July 18).

Reavey, William. 1993. "New Health Care Programs Offering Coverage in Mexico Could Lower Costs for U.S. Firms." *U.S.-Mexico Free Trade Reporter* (November 19).

Robinson, Jerry. 1994. Director, City of Laredo Health Department, Laredo, Tex. Interview, December 7.

Rodriguez-Monroy, Daniel. 1994. "Perspectives and Trends in Private Health Coverage." Paper presented at a conference on "Health Care in Mexico: Infrastructure, Technologies, and Financing: Challenges and Opportunities." La Jolla, Calif. (July 19).

Rowland, Bob. 1994. "Crime Victim Spurned by Tijuana HMO." *San Diego Union-Tribune,* local edition (June 17).

Sánchez, Carolina. 1994. Promoción, Hospital de Especialidades, Nuevo Laredo, Tamaulipas. Interview, December 9.

Sánchez, Juan Daniel. 1995. "Sindicato y Pensiones, Pesadas Cargas de la Institution." *Epoca* (April 3).

Schneider, Paul. 1995. Vice President, E. J. Phelps and Company, San Diego, Calif. Telephone interview, May 11.

"Scramble for Places in a Growth Market." 1993. *Financial Times Business Reports* (October 8).

Seguros Monterrey Aetna. 1994. *Manual de Tarifas*. Mexico City. (January.)

Selwyn, B. J. 1993. *Epidemiological Issues in Family Health along the U.S.-Mexico Border.* Paper presented at a conference on "Foundation for the Future: The Health of the Family in the United States-Mexico Border." El Paso, Tex. (February).

Selwyn, B. J., et al. 1992. "A Binational Assessment of Maternal and Child Health Issues Using the Primary Health Care Review Approach: Cameron County, Texas, and Matamoros, Tamaulipas." *Border Health*, vol. 8, no. 3.

Servicios Medicos Internacionales (SMI). N.d. *Health Maintenance Plan*. San Diego, Calif. (Promotional material.)

Smith, J. C., C. W. Warren, and J. Nunez Garcia. 1983. *The U.S.-Mexico Border: Contraceptive Use and Maternal Health Care in Perspective, 1979.* El Paso, Tex.: United States-Mexico Border Health Association.

Soberon, Guillermo. 1994. "Options for the Development and Expansion of the Mexican Health Care System." Paper presented at a conference on "Health Care in Mexico: Infrastructure, Technologies, and Financing: Challenges and Opportunities." La Jolla, Calif. (July 18).

SourceMex. 1993a. "North American Free Trade Agreement: Summary of Developments." Economic News and Analysis on Mexico, Latin American Database. (January 20.)

———. 1993b. "U.S. Companies Form Partnerships with Mexican Firms to Gain Access to Latin American Insurance Market." Economic News and Analysis on Mexico, Latin American Database. (September 8.)

Texas Department of Insurance. 1995. *Current and Projected Activities in the Mexican Market and with Mexican Health Care Providers*. Survey. (January 28.)

Thompson, William W. 1993. "Cross-Border Health Care Utilization and Practices of Mexican-Americans in the Lower Rio Grande Valley." *Border Health*, vol. IX, no. 2 (Apr., May, June).

Torres Cross, Sergio. 1992. "Benefits in Mexico: Facing the Future." *Employee Benefits Journal* (December).

United Communications Group. 1993. "Finance: Social Security Tax Battle." Available from Mexico Service, LEXIS/NEXIS (August 8).

U.S. Congress. Senate. 1993. *United States-Mexico Border Health Commission Act.* 103rd Cong., 1st sess., S. 1255.

Warner, David, and Kevin Reed. 1993. *Health Care across the Border: The Experience of U.S. Citizens in Mexico.* Lyndon B. Johnson School of Public Affairs, U.S.-Mexican Policy Studies Program, no. 4. Austin, Tex.

"Why Insurers Are Splashing across the Rio Grande." 1993. *Business Week* (August 9).

William M. Mercer, Inc. 1992. *International Country Reference Guide on Mexico.* New York. (November.)

———. 1995. *1995 Mexico Seminars: Compensation and Benefit Issues.* New York. (April 6.)

"World Corporate Insurance Reports." 1995. *Financial Times Limited* (May 19).

Zavaleta, Tony, et al. 1985. "Health Needs Assessment Survey for Brownsville: A U.S.-Mexico Border Community Case Study, 1983-1985." Brownsville, Tex.

Zinnecker, Anita Kuhl. 1990. "Health along the Texas-Mexico Border: Insights on the Utilization of Health Services by Mexican Nationals." Professional Report, Lyndon B. Johnson School of Public Affairs, The University of Texas at Austin.